The Issues of Life

Questions & Answers with God

By Edward A. Luongo

The King in his Beauty Books 2022

Text Copyright © by Edward A. Luongo

The King in his Beauty Books 2022

Dedication

This book is dedicated to my Lord and Saviour Jesus Christ. It is my desire that it would in some way be used by him to bring glory to his name.

I also dedicate this work to my beloved wife. She is a constant reminder of God's faithfulness and love for me. I am blessed to have her in my life. She is a virtuous woman and a crown to this blessed man.

And finally, I wish to dedicate this small work to all those who have questions that they would like answered. May your inquisitive mind lead you to the true source of knowledge; Jesus Christ...through the word of God.

Table of Contents

Introduction

People are filled with questions. We were created with an inquisitive mind and a desire to know. As with many things in life, this can be both good or bad. Sometimes we don't think of the desire to know as ever possibly being bad or dangerous. But it was Eve's desire to know hidden knowledge (the knowledge of good and evil) that caused her to disobey God, and fall into sin in the Garden of Eden.

Over the years I have attended many seminars and business meetings. I have heard presenters say things like, "the only dumb question is the one you don't ask", or "there are no dumb questions".

Is this true; are there no dumb questions? Are some questions more valid than others, or are they all the same?

I would like to explore some of life's most important questions from the Bible...from God's point of view. In this book I will examine questions that are asked and answered in the Bible. Some of these questions will be questions people have asked of God, and some will be questions God has asked of his Creation, you and me. You will likely find some of the questions that you or your loved one has asked at one time or another.

This book can, and preferably should be, read from start to finish as I have attempted to structure truth built upon truth in some logical format. However, it also lends itself as a quick reference to specific questions that can be read in any order.

May you find God's answers to your "Issues of Life" and may you learn to seek His wisdom from the Holy Bible. Use this book as a starting point to dig deeper into the Holy Bible and the issues of life.

Keep thy heart with all diligence; for out of it are the issues of life.
(Proverbs 4:23)

Chapter 1
<u>Beginnings</u>

The Foundations of Knowledge

As human beings we learn new things all the time. We call those things that we learn, knowledge, the accumulation of our knowing. But how do we learn? We learn in one of three primary ways. While we can learn some things of God's nature by Observation and Reason, it will be by Revelation that we will learn what God has to say to us.

I mention this upfront because God is a Spirit and therefore unseen by our human eyes. But He has been revealed to us just the same. He shows us his power in Creation with the Earth, Sun, Moon and Stars...all the great heavenly bodies in perfect relationship to each other to support life. He proved his existence to us and love for us on the Cross of Calvary...the single greatest act of compassion...and is further proven by various historical accounts many times over.

Observation: From observation we make judgments and acquire knowledge. Observation is at the heart of true science. We experiment through observation and record what we learn. Most of us love this method of learning because as the old saying goes; "Seeing is believing". And yet, we may observe and still not believe.

Reason: God has given us the ability to reason about things we cannot observe. This permeates the field of Theoretical ("higher") Mathematics. Sometimes we reason that if one thing is true then a certain other thing may also be true. Reason occurs in the realm of the mind and can't always be observed.

Revelation: Revelation is that knowledge which has been handed down to us in some manner. For instance, God gave us revelation about himself through the Holy Bible. Although we can look up into the heavens and wonder at the great Creator who made all the stars and planets, it is only by God's direct revelation that we can learn the details of who he is. This is the **spiritual realm**; things which may not be able to be observed or reasoned on its own...but every bit as real.

It is to this Revelation from God that we will turn over and over again for the answers to our questions about **The Issues of Life**.

Question 1
<u>Is God Real?</u>

Let's start off with a simple but profound question; Is God real and does he exist? Yes, God is real...but I can't "prove" his existence to you. There are many different thoughts as to how to go about proving God's existence, but in the end, it will require faith. Now, this is not **"blind faith"** as some may call it. I like to call it a **"step of faith"**. When you step out by faith and accept the reality of God with a sincere heart attitude, he will step out to meet you and confirm that faith in many ways. He will prove himself to you over and over again as you trust him and honestly seek him. And once you accept God's existence you will be amazed at the accuracy of the bible in such fields as science, philosophy, prophecy and human nature.

I never run from the fact that it requires faith to believe that God is real. Many things in life require faith to one degree or another. For instance, when you get a diagnosis from the doctor of cancer and he offers you a treatment plan it requires some measure of faith to proceed with his recommendation. Afterall, you don't fully understand the disease and the treatment, and so you proceed with some amount of faith... and yes, hope.

One of the easiest proofs of God's existence is the **reality of life**. We exist not by cosmic accident but by the will of God. Not matter what (some) scientists like to say about the theory of evolution, **nothing evolves**. You cannot point out any creature that is in some stage of evolutionary development today. Why not? Even if evolution requires millions of years to see the evidence, where is the creature today that began its evolutionary process a few million years ago. There aren't any...**and that's a fact!** What (some) scientists may call evolution is often simple adaptation of a species to its changing environment, utilizing the information already contained in its complex DNA and gene structure.

Let me layout a few formulas for life and see if one doesn't make more sense than the others.

The Evolutionist gives the formula for life as:

Nothing + Chance + Time = Life

This is an impossible equation for life, simply for the fact that "Nothing" is impossible; "Nothing" does not exist. Nothing means "No Thing", which is impossible. So, we could rewrite their formula as:

Matter + Chance + Time = Life

With this formula we must now accept that Matter is somehow eternal and has always been here. Does that make more sense than believing that an Eternal Creator was the one who created life? But, if you believe that matter had no beginning, then that matter somehow brought forth life. Pretty hard to swallow if you ask me.

Another theory put forth by evolutionists for life without a Creator (God) is called Panspermia; the idea that aliens from another dimension or universe, seeded life here and then left. Of course, there is absolutely no proof for this thought, but it is out there as an explanation for life. Oh, by the way, if that were true, what was the origin of their existence?

8

The Bible gives a clear and straight forward statement about the creation of the universe and life itself. The formula is simple.

An Eternal God = Created Life

First, God created all the elements required for life. The Bible says; *"In the beginning God created the heaven and the earth"*. In that simple statement we find **God** (the source of the power or energy needed), **Time** (in the beginning), **Space** (heaven) and **Matter** (earth). These are all the building blocks needed to create and sustain life; you can't have the one without the other! After this we read; *"So God created man in his own image, in the image of God created he him; male and female created he them"*.

So, if you examine the choices for the origin of life you find that there are very few options, and only one really makes sense. Here are those choices once more:
- Nothing (No Thing) created life.
- Eternal matter created life.
- Aliens (what was their origin?) created life.
- God (An eternal, all powerful being) created life

It is unreasonable to say on the one hand that a house requires a designer and builder (creator), but complex human and animal life does not.

For those who do not believe in an all-powerful and eternal God I say, prove he does **not** exist. Unless you have been everywhere in the Universe, you can't say there is no God. The evidence is all around you and the burden to disprove God's existence is on you. And prove it with the same standards that you would have me prove God to you! Again, I say, everything, to one extent or another, requires faith.

For those who are willing to accept that there is a Creator God let me encourage you; that same God became a man that he might provide eternal life for you. That God-Man's name is Jesus, the Christ and Saviour of the world. Jesus said; *Let not your heart be troubled: ye believe in God, <u>believe also in me</u>.*

Question 2
<u>Is Jesus a man or God?</u>

This is actually a very important question. The short answer is, according to the Bible, Jesus was both man and God. Jesus asked his disciples one day about this very matter. Here is some of that account from the gospel of Matthew.

> *Matthew 16:13 When Jesus came into the coasts of Caesarea Philippi, he asked his disciples, saying, Whom do men say that I the Son of man am? 14 And they said, Some say that thou art John the Baptist: some, Elias; and others, Jeremias, or one of the prophets.*

In other words, some people say you are simply a man, maybe a great man, but just a man. This same argument goes on today. Some see Jesus as simply a peaceful prophet who was a good man, but not God. But the account continues.

> *15 He saith unto them, But whom say ye that I am? 16 And Simon Peter answered and said, Thou art the Christ, the Son of the living God.*

Peter has answered correctly, and in the verses which follow, Jesus tells him just that. The Bible leaves us with no doubt as to this question; Jesus was both man and God. He wasn't half man and half God. He was fully a man and fully God; he was Immanuel, which means "God with us". This may not be easy to understand but it is easy to believe by faith. The same God who created everything is the same God who presented himself as a man for a short time on earth.

The reality is, only a man who was also God could accomplish the payment for mankind's sins.

There is a Law in the Old Testament called the Law of the Kinsman Redeemer *(Leviticus 25:25-28)*, given to the people of Israel. It stated that a near kin (relative) could redeem or buy back the property of an impoverished relative. This is a picture of what Jesus did when he redeemed us from our sins and the just punishment of those sins, when he died on the cross of Calvary. But in order for Jesus to fulfill the Law of the Kinsman Redeemer he had to become <u>near to us</u>. Only as a man could God himself become a kinsman to us.

In the case of mankind, the Kinsman Redeemer must also be God however. It would require a sinless life *(Hebrews 4:15)* and God's own blood *(Acts 20:28)* to pay the debt of the sins of the whole world.

So, only as God in the flesh, could the Law of the Kinsman Redeemer be fulfilled and mankind be set free from the bondage and penalty of sin, by faith in the Son of God.

Question 3
Is the Bible Trustworthy?

There are those who believe that the Bible is a collection of fairy tales or perhaps allegories, written my men and designed to teach a moral lesson. The Bible does contain some allegories and parables, but those are identified as such in Scripture. By the way, a parable is a story designed to teach spiritual truth in a manner that most people could relate to. In other words, parables aren't fairy tales at all. The Bible is first and foremost, a book, written by an author (God) to communicate and reveal truth to the reader. It can and should be taken literally in context, unless the text itself identifies a passage as a parable or allegory. The Bible also contains symbols which stand for something other than what is described. These too are so identified in the text. For instance, in the Book of Revelation we find the mention of candlesticks, which are later identified as representing Churches that existed during the time of the writing of Revelation.

There are many ways to examine the issue of the Bible's trustworthiness, and thus its truthfulness. First, let's see what the Bible says about itself.

> *Thy word is true from the beginning: and every one of thy righteous judgments endureth for ever. (Psalm 119:160)*

> *Every word of God is pure: he is a shield unto them that put their trust in him. (Proverbs 30:5)*

Some are under the wrong impression that men wrote the Bible. However, the Bible declares that God, through his Holy Spirit, is the author of the Bible. God used men to write down the words that he gave them, and therefore, the Bible contains the words of God, not men.

For the prophecy came not in old time by the will of man: but holy men of God spake as they were moved by the Holy Ghost. (2 Peter 1:21)

All scripture is given by inspiration of God, and is profitable for doctrine, for reproof, for correction, for instruction in righteousness: (2 Timothy 3:16)

For this cause also thank we God without ceasing, because, when ye received the word of God which ye heard of us, ye received it not as the word of men, but as it is in truth, the word of God, which effectually worketh also in you that believe. (1 Thessalonians 2:13)

I have it heard it said that a good man would not write the Bible because he was good and **would** not lie and say that he wrote it, and that an evil man **could** not write the Bible because he was evil and the Bible is good.

In this section I want to briefly examine the accuracy and trustworthiness of the Bible in various disciplines of Science, Psychology, History and Prophecy. It is my hope that these few examples will give you confidence to step out in that first step of faith and believe that Jesus Christ is who he said he was, and that his word is true from start to finish. Remember, faith is not a cop out; faith is what is required to believe and it is that which pleases God!

Science

Here are some interesting facts from the Bible which predate all the scientists. Though not always given with a lot of detail, it can still be seen that the Bible was miraculously ahead of science by many years. Obviously, the author of the Bible was God himself, not man.

Medical Science: Washing with Running Water

The first example has to do with the importance of washing with running water for good hygiene and disease prevention. In the year 1846 a Hungarian doctor named Ignaz Semmelweis determined that the washing of hands and medical instruments under running water could prevent infections from spreading. Remember, running water is needed for cleansing; just rinsing your hands in stationary water is not enough.

In B.C. 1490 (over 3000 years prior), the Bible teaches the importance of washing under running water for the cleaning of disease. Quoting from *Leviticus 15:13*; *And when he that hath an issue is cleansed of his issue; then he shall number to himself seven days for his cleansing, and <u>wash his clothes, and bathe his flesh in running water, and shall be clean</u>.* So, centuries before medical doctors began to understand the link between washing with running water and disease prevention, the Bible held the key to this modern-day practice.

Medical Science: Importance of the Blood for Life

For centuries doctors used a medical procedure called "bloodletting" where leeches were used to "drain" blood from the patient to cure various diseases. Much harm was done to the patient through this practice, and some even died from the loss of blood.

But in B.C. 1490 the Bible taught the importance of the blood to sustain life with a simple but profound statement of absolute medical fact; *Leviticus 17:11 For the life of the flesh is in the blood:*
Only the Creator could know such a thing thousands of years before medical science figured this out. You see, the blood carries the oxygen and energy to every cell of your body. If you lose too much blood or if the blood gets severely infected, you can die.

The Science of Astronomy: The Earth "Floats" in the Air

For many years various societies believed that the earth was held up by Atlas or on the back of a turtle or elephant. In B.C. 1520 the Bible declared that the earth was not supported by anything like so many believed, but was actually hanging upon nothing (which we now call gravitational force).

He stretcheth out the north over the empty place, and hangeth the earth upon nothing. (Job 26:7)

The Science of Astronomy: The Earth is a Circle or Sphere

We now know that the earth is in the shape of a circle or sphere. But for many years scientists believed that the earth was flat. In B.C. 700 the Prophet Isaiah declared; *It is he that sitteth upon the <u>circle of the earth</u>, and the inhabitants thereof are as grasshoppers; that stretcheth out the heavens as a curtain, and spreadeth them out as a tent to dwell in: (Isaiah 40:22)*

The Science of Astronomy: The Stars are Innumerable

Years ago, Astronomers would count the stars and came up with various numbers for how many stars were in the heavens. The answers they came up with were usually just a few thousand. Obviously, we know today from telescopes and satellite images that the actual number is too many to count. Once again, the Bible was years ahead of the scientists for it declares in *Genesis 22:17 That in blessing I will bless thee, and in multiplying I will multiply thy seed as the stars of the heaven, and as the sand which is upon the sea shore; and thy seed shall possess the gate of his enemies;*
From this verse we see that the Bible likens the number of stars to the number of the grains of sand on the sea shore; in other words, innumerable!

The Science of Meteorology: Circuits of the Wind

Modern Meteorologists know all about the circuits that the wind travels but the Bible gave us this information around B.C. 1000.

> *The wind goeth toward the south, and turneth about unto the north; it whirleth about continually, and the wind returneth again according to his circuits. (Ecclesiastes 1:6)*

The Science of Meteorology: Hydro Cycle

Here is the Bible describing the rain and evaporation cycle in B.C. 700.

> *Ecclesiastes 1:7 All the rivers run into the sea; yet the sea is not full; unto the place from whence the rivers come, thither they return again.*

The Science of Oceanography: Springs of the Ocean

The oceans are very deep, and much today is still unknown and unexplored about them. And yet the Patriarch, Job, knew that the ocean depths contained springs of water that would help to replenish the waters of the oceans. This modern-day discovery did not take place until 1970, almost 3500 years after Job declared it.

> *Job 38:16 Hast thou entered into the springs of the sea? or hast thou walked in the search of the depth?*

The Science of Oceanography: Mountains Under Sea

Who would have guessed that under the oceans lay huge mountain ranges? It is only in the past century that man has discovered this fact through underwater exploration. And yet, the

Prophet Jonah declared that there were mountains under the sea in B.C. 1500.

> *Jonah 2:5 The <u>waters</u> compassed me about, even to the soul: the depth closed me round about, the weeds were wrapped about my head. 6 I went down to the bottoms of the <u>mountains</u>; the earth with her bars was about me for ever: yet hast thou brought up my life from corruption, O LORD my God.*

The Science of Physics: Unseen Particles

Reality exists at the sub-atomic level; that which is invisible to the naked eye, and only "visible" as patterns splashed across Atom Splitters. But the Bible "hints" that all of Creation is made up of things which cannot be seen, i.e., atomic particles.

> *Hebrews 11:3 Through faith we understand that the worlds were framed by the word of God, so that things which are seen were not made of things which do appear.*

Psychology

The Bible accurately discusses the interconnectedness of the mind and body; the spiritual with the physical. Modern day Psychologists try to understand and assess the inner emotions of people, but often do so without the advantage of believing the "Owner's Manual" for humanity; the Holy Bible.

Here are just a few of the insights into human nature that we get from the Bible. The Bible addresses the issues of life and the thoughts of the heart like no other book can or does.

The Bible teaches that the important issues of our life are a matter of the inner being, indicating that people are far more than just physical beings directed only by the chemical workings of the brain.

Keep thy heart with all diligence; for out of it are the issues of life. (Proverbs 4:23)

As every good advertising agency knows, the things we look at affect the way we feel on the inside and often act on the outside. Far more important however than just trying to affect the things we purchase; God instructs us that we should be careful of the things that we view with our eyes because of the interconnectedness of physical (eyes) with the inner issues of the heart and emotions.

Mine eye affecteth mine heart because of all the daughters of my city. (Lamentations 3:51)

I offer just one more of the many examples from the Bible in this area of Psychology.

A merry heart maketh a cheerful countenance: but by sorrow of the heart the spirit is broken. (Proverbs 15:13)

Once again, we see the relation between our inner spiritual being and our physical being. If you look carefully at this verse, you find hinted at something which very few Psychologists recognize; that is, the three-fold nature of a person. In this verse you find the essence of a person in body, soul and spirit.

- **Body**; countenance
- **Soul**; the heart, which is the seat of our emotions
- **Spirit**; the seat of our will

If we don't recognize the true three-fold nature of a person and the interconnectedness of the "inner" person with the "outer" person, how can we ever hope to truly help people and meet their greatest needs?

History

The Bible is a book whose people and places have been literally "dug out of the ground". There have been numerous archaeological discoveries that prove the accuracy of the Biblical accounts. I will give just a couple of examples, but please note, there are many more. These discoveries attest to the accuracy of the history as presented in the Bible, and therefore, the Bible itself.

In 1835 Sir Henry Rawlinson, a British army officer discovered carvings on the smooth surface of a rock in the Behistun mountain, 200 miles Northeast of Babylon. When he investigated the carvings, he read an inscription engraved, B.C. 516, by order of king Darius of Persia (521-485 B.C.). This is the same Darius under whom the Temple of Jerusalem was rebuilt according to the Book of Ezra in the Bible.

I will give just one more example to illustrate my point. There is a stone tablet known as Annipadda's Foundation Tablet. It was discovered by Wooley in 1923. The Tablet is approximately 3 by 4 inches. The inscription says; *"Annipadda, king of Ur, son of Messanipadda, has built for his lady Nin-Kharsag"*. This archeological find, and others like it, confirms the existence of Ur, known in the Bible as the land from which Abraham travelled (Ur of the Chaldees; Genesis 11:31).

Prophecy

For the testimony of Jesus is the spirit of prophecy (Revelation 19:10)

Prophecy is history told in advance of the event; it is telling the future. The Bible, and no other religious or secular book, has hundreds of very specific prophecies that have already come to pass. There is no way for a human being to predict the future with such accuracy and specificity as we find in the Scriptures. In this section I will briefly lay out some of the very specific prophecies contained in the Bible about the life of Jesus Christ.

Another fruitful study of prophecy concerns the Nation of Israel. While we won't examine that here, just know, God foretold a time when he would disperse Israel throughout the world but then bring them back to their ancestral land in the latter days; this began with the statehood of Israel in 1948. An amazing prophecy!

These events could not have been arranged by men since the Bible was written over a period of around 1500 years by 40 plus different (human) writers that did not know each other. There was no conspiracy to deceive!

Prophecy is given in Scripture to show that God knows the end from the beginning and to give us confidence in Him and his word, the Holy Bible.

> *Now I tell you before it come, that, <u>when it is come to pass, ye may believe that I am he</u>. (John 13:19)*

Prophecies Concerning Jesus Christ:

There is no doubt historically that a man named Jesus lived some 2000 years ago. There are many historical records both inside and outside of the Bible that attest to this fact. The only question really is, was he actually the Son of God as he claimed to be. Well, certainly, the Bible declares him to be God in the flesh, and, as we shall see, Prophecy confirms the validity of Christ's deity.

There are several hundred prophecies in the Old Testament concerning the birth, life, death and resurrection of Jesus Christ. Those wishing to examine this point further just need to visit a Christian bookstore or go online and query; "Prophecies Concerning Jesus Christ". Below I present just a few of these prophecies to show how specific they were and how Jesus fulfilled them exactly as foretold.

20

The Old Testament was completed over 400 years before Jesus was born. It contains over 300 prophecies that Jesus fulfilled through His birth, life, death and resurrection.

Mathematically, the odds of anyone fulfilling all these prophecies are staggering. Mathematicians put it this way:

- **1 person fulfilling 8 prophecies: 1 in 100,000,000,000,000,000**
- **1 person fulfilling 48 prophecies: 1 chance in 10 to the 157th power. This number is so staggeringly large that it is more in number than all the electrons in the known universe...yea, really!**
- **1 person fulfilling 300+ prophecies: IMPOSSIBLE, unless God wrote the Bible**

His Birth:

In B.C. 710 the Prophet Micah wrote; *But thou, Bethlehem Ephratah, though thou be little among the thousands of Judah, yet out of thee shall he come forth unto me that is to be ruler in Israel; whose goings forth have been from of old, from everlasting. (Micah 5:2)* Here is the prophecy concerning a future ruler of Israel who would be *"from everlasting"* (eternal, without beginning or ending). He is said to come from Bethlehem Ephratah, the exact place of Jesus' birth *(Matthew 2:1-6)*. The prophecy was so specific that it mentions Ephratah, which is important when you consider that at the time of Jesus' birth there were two cities by the name of Bethlehem!

His Life:

In B.C. 740 the Prophet Hosea wrote a prophecy about a child that would be loved by God, and at some point, called out of Egypt. Now historically this speaks to Israel as a nation; birthed by God, sent into Egypt for 400 years and called out by God in the Exodus from Egypt. But prophetically, it speaks to Jesus as the only begotten of the

Father, who would go into Egypt only to be latter called out by God. You see the fulfillment of this prophecy in Matthew's gospel account.

> *Matthew 2:13 And when they were departed, behold, the angel of the Lord appeareth to Joseph in a dream, saying, Arise, and take the young child and his mother, and flee into Egypt, and be thou there until I bring thee word: for Herod will seek the young child to destroy him. 14 When he arose, he took the young child and his mother by night, and departed into Egypt: 15 And was there until the death of Herod: that it might be fulfilled which was spoken of the Lord by the prophet, saying, Out of Egypt have I called my son.*

The prophets warned that someone who had been a very close friend to Jesus would betray him *(Psalm 41:9)* for 30 pieces of silver, which would later be used to buy a potter's field *(Zechariah 11:12-13)*. Upon His betrayal, the Messiah's closest friends would flee from him *(Psalm 31:11)*.

> *Zechariah 11:12 And I said unto them, If ye think good, give me my price; and if not, forbear. So they weighed for my price thirty pieces of silver. 13 And the LORD said unto me, Cast it unto the potter: a goodly price that I was prised at of them. And I took the thirty pieces of silver, and cast them to the potter in the house of the LORD.*

This is exactly what we find happening in the life of Jesus hundreds of years after these prophecies were made. We read in the gospels of...

Jesus being betrayed by one of his close friends and apostle, Judas, for 30 pieces of silver. *Matthew 26:14 Then one of the twelve, called Judas Iscariot, went unto the chief priests,*

> *15 And said unto them, What will ye give me, and I will deliver him unto you? And they covenanted with him for*

thirty pieces of silver. 16 And from that time he sought opportunity to betray him.

We see also his closest friends (disciples) flee from him as the Prophet said. The gospel account of *Mark 14:50* simply says; *And they all forsook him, and fled.*

His Death:
The Prophet Isaiah tells how the Messiah would remain silent even while being falsely accused and that he would be beaten, mocked, and spat upon *(Isaiah 53:7; Isaiah 50:6)*. The Savior would also be *"wounded for our transgressions and pierced for our iniquities"* so that by His stripes (wounds) we would be healed *(Isaiah 53:5)*.

In the Psalms of King David, we find further details concerning Jesus' death. David prophesied that the Messiah's hands and feet would be pierced but His bones would not be broken *(Psalm 22:16-17; 34:20)*. The Psalmist said that people would cast lots for His clothing *(Psalm 22:18)* and that onlookers would mock Jesus by telling him to ask the God to rescue him *(Psalm 22:8)*.

Isaiah once again weighed in when he wrote that the Savior would die among criminals *(Isaiah 53:9)*.

These prophecies were 100% fulfilled in the manner and detail that the prophets wrote about hundreds of years before they took place.

Anyone familiar with Jesus' death knows that He fulfilled the prophecies of the Messiah's death down to the last detail. Specifically, Jesus remained silent in the face of false accusations, and was beaten, mocked, and spat upon before His crucifixion as fulfilled in *(Mark 14:57-61; 15:16-20)*.

Further, the Savior's hands and feet were pierced by nails at His crucifixion, but his bones left unbroken *(Luke 24:39-40; John 20:24-*

27; John 19:33-37). As prophesied, two criminals were crucified beside Jesus *(Mark 15:27-28)*, and Roman soldiers cast lots for His garments *(John 19:23-24)*. And finally, we find fulfilled the prophecy that he would be mocked and scorned to save himself from death in order to prove he really was who he said he was *(Luke 23:35)*.

His Resurrection:

King David, writing around B.C. 1000, prophesied that God would not abandon Jesus after his death by leaving him in Hell or let his body remain in the tomb long enough to decay *(Psalm 16:10)*. David also wrote that Jesus would ascend to Heaven and sit at God's right hand *(Psalm 110:1)*.

Isaiah further divined that the Messiah's death would serve as an ultimate offering for sin so that God's people could be redeemed *(Isaiah 53:5-12)*. The Messiah's agony would be rewarded, however, in that He'd conquer death in the end *(Isaiah 25:7-8)* and *"see the light of life and be satisfied"* (Isaiah 53:11).

As prophesied, Jesus conquered death by gloriously rising from the dead *(Matthew 28:5-10)*. He then appeared to many of His disciples *(Matthew 28:16-17)* who later testified that the he had risen, that His body was without decay, and that He had ascended into Heaven to sit at the right hand of God, as prophesied *(Acts 2:24-36)*.

The resurrection of Jesus Christ is obviously a big deal. There has never been a claim of something like this ever happening before or since. It is so important to the good news of the Gospel of Jesus Christ and Christianity as a whole, that the Apostle Paul wrote; *But if there be no resurrection of the dead, then is Christ not risen: And if Christ be not risen, then is our preaching vain, and your faith is also vain. (1 Corinthians 15:13-14)*

The Apostle Paul was one of those living at the time of the resurrection and would know for sure whether or not the resurrection was real or not. Others also, such as, the Apostle Peter,

24

would have been aware of whether or not the account was true. These same men, and many others, were so convinced of the resurrection (<u>because they saw Jesus after he was resurrected</u>) that it changed them completely. They went preaching the Good News that Jesus had risen from the dead and offered eternal life to those that would believe in him.

So, the very people who would have known whether the resurrection was true or a lie, declared it was true. And many of them would eventually be martyred for that belief. These men and woman who saw Jesus after his resurrection knew it was true, and so were willing to give their lives for the truth.

For a further discussion of the fact of the resurrection please see the wonderful book by Harvard law professor, Simon Greenleaf titled, The Testimony of the Evangelists.

Question 4
Which Bible Should I Read?

There are many versions of the Bible available online and at any bookstore. You may wonder if they are all the same or is one better than the other. Years ago, I was curious about this very thing and began a careful examination of the issue. Here is what I found.

First, all the Bible versions are not the same in many places. Some have fewer verses than others and some have more. At first this may seem confusing to you, but don't let that scare you off. For as long as the word of God has existed, there are those who would attempt to corrupt it. The very first "higher critic" of the Bible was none other than Satan himself. It was he who first said; *"Yea, hath God said..."* in *Genesis 3:1*. Of course, since then, Satan has had help in corrupting the words of God by certain men over the centuries. You see, the Devil wants to destroy your confidence in the Bible because it is the best "weapon" we have to fight off his lies.

So, it is important for me to take some time to discuss this issue. For English speaking people, the only Bible I would recommend is the Authorized 1611, King James Bible. Other Bible versions have been corrupted by the original "higher critic" of God's word (Satan) and his *"ministers" (2 Corinthians 11:15).* Perhaps the two most influential men in this corruption process were Bishop Brooke Foss Westcott (1825-1903) and Fenton John Anthony Hort (1828-1892). These two men chaired what was supposed to be a revision of the King James Bible. In reality, it was not really a revision of the King James Bible, but a new translation altogether. Utilizing two very corrupt Manuscripts, Sinaiticus and Vaticanus they produced the corrupt English Revised Version of 1881-1884. These two manuscripts form the basis for most of the corruption that has taken place in the modern English translations we have today (New International Version, New American Standard Version, etc....).

From even a brief examination of Sinaiticus and Vaticanus it becomes very obvious that these two Manuscripts had been altered in many places, making them corrupt and untrustworthy. Westcott and Hort were two unsaved men, the likes of which we are warned about in *2 Corinthians 11:15.* They disguised themselves as ministers of righteousness, when in fact they were ministers of Satan. If you were to read their biographies you would find that these men did not believe in important biblical doctrines, such as, a literal Heaven and Hell.

> *2 Corinthians 2:17 For we are not as many, which corrupt the word of God: ...*

I will give you just one of many examples that highlight the corruption that has taken place in the modern versions; the doctrine of the Trinity.

The doctrine of the Godhead (Trinity) is central to the Christian faith. It states that there is one God in the three equal persons of the Father, Son and Holy Ghost. Take a look at the comparisons below to see a prime example of the corruption that has taken place. The scripture verse is from *1 John 5:7-8*.

King James Bible	English Revised Version	New International Version	New American Standard
For there are three that bear record in heaven, the Father, the Word, and the Holy Ghost: <u>and these three are one.</u>	And the Spirit is the witness, because the Spirit is the truth. There are three witnesses, the Spirit, the water, and the blood; and these three agree.	For there are three that testify: the Spirit, the water and the blood; and the three are in agreement.	For there are three that testify: the Spirit, the water and the blood; and the three are in agreement.

In each of the three versions above you can plainly see how the all-important doctrine of the Trinity has disappeared when compared to the King James Bible. Unfortunately, this is just the beginning of the corruption that has taken place over the years.

If you care to examine this topic in detail there are many excellent resources that can be looked at. Here are three excellent books on this subject:
1. New Age Bible Versions by Gail Riplinger
2. Understandable History of the Bible by Samuel Gipp
3. Which Version is the Bible by Floyd Nolen Jones

Chapter 2
Five Big Questions for God

In this chapter I would like to consider some important questions that many people ask sincerely, and to which they deserve an answer. My answers will be based on my understanding of the Bible. I believe the Bible contains the answers to life's questions and can be fully relied upon as trustworthy. The very God of Heaven desires you to know truth. He said in his Word; *"Come now, let us reason together, saith the LORD…".*

The writer of the Book of Proverbs said; *Keep thy heart with all diligence; for out of it are the issues of life.*

Here is an important reminder from the Bible that the issues of our life come from our heart, our inner being of personality and emotions. As such, we can gain great insight from the Bible because it is a spiritual book, speaking to the inner being. The Bible is unlike any book when it comes to understanding human nature and the innermost needs of people. This is so because the Bible was written by God, using men as the instruments to record and preserve his words.

The Bible says that it is able to "read" our hearts; quoting from *Hebrews 4:12* we find; *For the word of God is quick, and powerful, and sharper than any twoedged sword, piercing even to the dividing asunder of soul and spirit, and of the joints and marrow, and is a discerner of the thoughts and intents of the heart.*

So, let's begin this chapter with what I call the "Big Five" questions; (1) where did I come from, (2) does God have a purpose for my life, (3) what happens to me when I die (4) when I die, will I live again and (5) what must I do to inherit eternal life?

These questions may not be asked in this manner or with these particular words, but they are key questions that are on the minds of many people. For instance, someone may not ask; "what happens to me when I die"? They may simply say that they are afraid of dying...which is not a question at all...but it is still a desire to know the truth of the matter.

Question 1
Where Did I Come From?

To answer this question, we will first look at the Evolutionary Theory of life. I want to examine the Theory of Evolution just to point out that it is impossible for life to come from nothing.

We will then examine the biblical account of Creation for life.

(a) The Evolutionary Account

Let me remind you that the Evolutionists have multiple theories for the origin of life. This of course means, **they don't actually know the origin of life**! No matter what you hear and read in support of evolution, it has never been proven, it has never been observed...and it never will be. Rather, the Evolutionist starts off with the notion; "There is no God, therefore...". They may not say it just that way but that is the root of their thinking, that is, God does not exist, and therefore there must be another explanation for life. This is "convenient" for someone who does not want to be accountable to their Creator.

There are many, many fine books that discuss in detail the significant errors and problems with the theory of evolution, you just have to look for them in Christian bookstores or Christian websites. I can make one book recommendation, and that is all you will really need. There is an excellent book called The Evolution Handbook, available at evolutionfacts.com. It is inexpensive and very detailed. You won't be disappointed.

Evolutionists believe certain principles that are contrary to common sense itself.

1. They believe that the natural laws we find evident in nature somehow sprang into existence on their own, out of designless confusion and chaos.
2. They believe that matter sprang into existence on its own or perhaps matter is somehow eternal itself.
3. They believe that non-living matter somehow produced life, though this has NEVER been observed anywhere.

Obviously, none of this makes much common sense, let alone scientific sense.

Let's discuss briefly a few of the problems with their theory in general.

1. There is absolutely no proof for evolution, which is why they have several theories.
2. **NO ONE** has ever seen anything evolving. Evolution has never been observed and therefore cannot be subject to the scientific method for study; observation and testing.
3. **NO ONE** has ever produced life from matter in a laboratory setting or shown how it is even <u>mathematically</u> possible.
4. The fossil records show absolutely no transitional evolutionary process (as in a change from one form to another). Fossil records would be the only hope an Evolutionist has of providing evidence in support of their theory, but the fossils **DO NOT** support their theory.
5.   The Laws of Nature **DO NOT** support evolution. In science a Law is something that is beyond a Theory; it is something that has been proven and observed over and over again. Without great explanation let me lay two <u>Laws</u> of Nature before you:

The First Law of Thermodynamics is also called the Law of the Conservation of mass and energy. This Law states that "Energy cannot be created <u>by itself</u> nor destroyed. Energy may be changed from one form into another, but the total amount remains the same". In simple terms; matter cannot be   eliminated or created by itself. In other words, someone (God) had to create matter in the first place.

The Second Law of Thermodynamics is also called the Law of increasing entropy (increasing disorder). This Law states that in any system which contains information, the system "loses" information and becomes less ordered, or more random. Evolutionists say just the opposite; that life became more and more complex, not disordered and random. This is diametrically opposed to the observable Second Law of Thermodynamics. We know from experimental observation and the Bible itself, that our very universe is "winding down" and becoming more random, as the Second Law dictates. The Psalmist said; *Of old hast thou laid the foundation of the earth: and the heavens are the work of thy hands. They shall perish, but thou shalt endure: yea, all of them shall wax old like a garment; as a vesture shalt thou change them, and they shall be changed: (Psalm 102:25-26)*

(b) The Creation Account

This question gets to the heart of the Creation/Evolution debate. Did I really come out of the ocean in some amphibious form, only to eventually become a man or a woman? Or, was I part of a special plan of an all-powerful Creator?

The Bible is clear on this matter; God created a man (Adam) and a woman (Eve) and from them the whole world was populated. Jesus confirmed his belief in the Adam and Eve creation account in *Matthew 19:8*. God also created the heavens, earth, seas, stars, moon and all plant and animal life. There is no "which came first, the chicken or the egg" problem…the chicken came first, it was created.

Now, here are the scripture references that support these first claims:

Genesis 1:1 In the beginning God created the heaven and the earth.

Genesis 1:16 And God made two great lights; the greater light to rule the day, and the lesser light to rule the night: he made the stars also.

Genesis 1:24 And God said, Let the earth bring forth the living creature after his kind, cattle, and creeping thing, and beast of the earth after his kind: and it was so.

Genesis 1:27 So God created man in his own image, in the image of God created he him; male and female created he them.

So here we have it from God's point of view...nothing evolved, it was all part of his special Creation. Notice in the verses that follow the great care God took with his Creation of man and woman. He made them in his own image, provided food in the garden and gave them a purpose for their lives.

Gen 1:27 So God created man in his own image, in the image of God created he him; male and female created he them.

God made Adam and Eve to bear the very image of the Creator.

28 And God blessed them, and God said unto them, Be fruitful, and multiply, and replenish the earth, and subdue it: and have dominion over the fish of the sea, and over the fowl of the air, and over every living thing that moveth upon the earth. God blessed them and gave them purpose.

29 And God said, Behold, I have given you every herb bearing seed, which is upon the face of all the earth, and every tree, in the which is the fruit of a tree yielding seed; to you it shall be for meat. God provided food.

30 And to every beast of the earth, and to every fowl of the air, and to every thing that creepeth upon the earth, wherein there is life, I have given every green herb for meat: and it was so. 31 And God saw every thing that he had made, and, behold, it was very good. And the evening and the morning were the sixth day. God provided food for the animals and pronounced that everything was very good.

In conclusion; evolution has **NO** scientific support and makes **NO** (common) sense, and should be quickly dismissed as false science *(1 Timothy 6:20)*. Special Creation, by an all-powerful and eternal God makes absolute scientific, and common sense.

If you are interested, get the book I mentioned earlier in this chapter and study the 900 plus pages of important detail it presents.

Question 2
Does God Have a Purpose for my Life?

And let fall also some of the handfuls of purpose for her, and leave them, that she may glean them, and rebuke her not. (Ruth 2:16)

If God is real and the Bible trustworthy, what does God expect of me...and does he have a purpose for my life?

In simple terms, God is looking for a personal relationship with you. The very God of Creation wants you to know him in a sincere and meaningful way. He gave us his Bible (his Word) that we might read and learn of him. Further, he wants us to know, love and learn about his only begotten Son, the Lord Jesus Christ.

In order to begin a close walk with God, you must approach him in the manner in which he prescribed in Scripture, that is, through his Son. Listen to the words that Jesus spoke just before he went to the cross to die for the sins of humanity; *Let not your heart be troubled: ye believe in God, believe also in me (John 14:1)*. Jesus knew it was a good thing for people to believe in God (the Father), but he also knew that you must follow up that belief by faith in Him too. Jesus knew that salvation would be found in him and his work on the cross of Calvary. In that same account with his disciples that day, he followed up that great statement with an all-important one about himself and the way to God the Father in Heaven. Listen carefully to his words from *John 14:6; Jesus saith unto him, I am the way, the truth, and the life: no man cometh unto the Father, but by me.* You see, the way to a relationship with God in Heaven is through faith in Jesus Christ and his finished work of salvation on the cross.

The beginning of our relationship with God begins with belief in Jesus Christ and his Gospel. The Gospel of Jesus Christ is the true account of the Death, Burial and Resurrection of Jesus Christ, according to the Scriptures (*1 Corinthians 15:1-4*). This is the only way in which you can become a child of God; *For we are all children of God by faith in Christ Jesus (Galatians 3:26)*. If you have never put in faith in Jesus Christ and his Gospel, please stop now and consider the following verses:

8 But what saith it? The word is nigh thee, even in thy mouth, and in thy heart: that is, the word of faith, which we preach; 9 That if thou shalt confess with thy mouth the Lord Jesus, and shalt believe in thine heart that God hath raised him from the dead, thou shalt be saved. 10 For with the heart man believeth unto righteousness; and with the mouth confession is made unto salvation. 11 For the scripture saith, Whosoever believeth on him shall not be ashamed. 12 For there is no difference between the Jew and the Greek: for the same Lord over all is rich unto all that call upon him. 13 For whosoever shall call upon the name of the Lord shall be saved. (Romans 10:8-13).

Won't you call on the name of the Lord Jesus Christ now? Only you can make that choice. The same God of Heaven who wants to have a personal relationship with you will not force you to believe.

Most people at some point in their life want to know what their purpose in life is. People seek purpose in many ways and in many places. It is all about; "where do I fit in". It is a basic need that we share as fellow human beings. We want to fit in and to know that we are appreciated, loved and making a difference. And so, we seek purpose; purpose in a job, purpose in a child, purpose in a relationship, purpose in helping others or perhaps, even purpose in a hobby or sport.

Since God took the time and care to create me, does he have a purpose for my life...and if so, what might that be? Let's take a look together at the Bible for some answers.

Your purpose is derived from the fact that God wants to have a personal relationship with you! If you think about that for a moment you will see that is an amazing claim. Is it true? Yes, it is. The God who created everything from nothing, and man from the dust of the ground, wants to have a personal relationship with you. This is why he says; *"Come now, let us reason together, saith the LORD".* So, let's talk about it.

When God first created Adam and Eve in the Garden of Eden, he spoke directly to them. The Bible says that God spoke to Adam and told him; *"Be fruitful and multiply and replenish the earth" (Genesis 1:28).* Here we get to see the heart of God in wanting his new Creatures to be fruitful and productive. As you continue to read the early Genesis account you will find God giving Adam dominion (authority) over all of Creation. His expectation of Adam is that he would be a good steward of all He had given him to manage.

What about you; does God have a plan and purpose for your life? Yes, even before you were actually born into this world God knew you in the womb. The Psalmist prayed to God when he wrote; *I will praise thee; for I am fearfully and wonderfully made.* He recognized God's hand in making him who he was, with all of his unique characteristics.

God's desire for you is that you (first) seek to know him in a personal way. He then desires that each of us walk humbly with him by faith, do right according to the Scriptures, and show mercy to those around us.

He hath shewed thee, O man, what is good; and what doth the LORD require of thee, but to do justly, and to love mercy, and to walk humbly with thy God? (Micah 6:8)

When we seek to follow God humbly by faith, he will begin to add purpose to our lives; often in the form of ministry to others. If you are a child of God, you will never be truly satisfied with your Faith until you are serving God in some capacity. We most often serve God best when we serve others.

The first and most important purpose (ministry) he gives to all his children (Christians by faith), is the *"ministry of reconciliation"*.

17 Therefore if any man be in Christ, he is a new creature: old things are passed away; behold, all things are become new. 18 And all things are of God, who hath reconciled us to himself by Jesus Christ, and hath <u>given to us the ministry of reconciliation</u>; 19 To wit, that God was in Christ, reconciling the world unto himself, not imputing their trespasses unto them; and hath committed unto us the word of reconciliation. 20 Now then we are ambassadors for Christ, as though God did beseech you by us: we pray you in Christ's stead, be ye reconciled to God. (2 Corinthians 5:17)

The Bible is not just any book; it is the book or words of eternal life. There is no other book that can impart the knowledge of eternal life. The Apostle Peter recognized this early in his life when he spoke to Jesus and said: *"Thou hast the words of eternal life"*. God has given you the ministry purpose of bringing those same words (his Bible and the Gospel of Jesus Christ) to those who do not yet know and understand. You are to reconcile God's lost and wandering Creation to the Creator, by the Gospel. This is your responsibility and privilege as a child of God by faith. From this one purpose will flow many ministry opportunities, giving God-Directed purpose to your life.

God ordained the institution of the Church, which is a local assembly of like-minded bible believing Christians. There are so many opportunities to serve under the direction of this local assembly. You might find that God wants you to be a help to the shut-in or perhaps make a meal from someone who is sick. You might find yourself given opportunities to sing or play music.

The most important thing is that God wants you to be faithful to Him and his Word, to be fruitful in ministry for his glory and honor and to be involved in that *"ministry of reconciliation"*. So, I would encourage you to find a good, King James, bible-believing church to fellowship, to worship and to serve in. This is where you have the best opportunity to find that God-Given purpose you so long for.

Question 3
<u>What Happens to me When I Die?</u>

9 For all our days are passed away in thy wrath: we spend our years as a tale that is told. 10 The days of our years are threescore years and ten; and if by reason of strength they be fourscore years, yet is their strength labour and sorrow; for it is soon cut off, and we fly away. (Psalm 90:9-10)

Obviously, this is a question most of us wonder about and even worry about. People everywhere and in every period of history have had some sense of fear about dying. This is the snare of the Devil and he has used it to torture so many people over the years. But it does not need to be that way because Jesus conquered death when he rose from the grave. And Jesus said; *"Yet a little while, and the world seeth me no more; but ye see me: because I live, ye shall live also."*. We will come to this question of eternal life shortly. But first, let's address the question; "what happens to me when I die"?

To begin to answer this question we need to take a small step back to lay a little ground work.

The Bible teaches that each person is a three-part being; a soul, spirit and body *(1 Thessalonians 5:23)*. We learn this first however in the book of *Genesis 2:7*, where we read *"And the LORD God formed man of the <u>dust</u> of the ground, and breathed into his nostrils the <u>breath of life</u>; and man became a living <u>soul</u>"*. To understand what happens to a person when they die, we must understand this three-fold nature. Let's take a look at this further.

The body is the house for the inner being of spirit and soul. The spirit and soul are not identical which is why the word of God (Bible) is able "divide" between the two *(Hebrews 4:12)*. The spirit is that active part of the mind which "knows" *(1 Corinthians 2:11)*, while the soul is that part which is the "seat" of our emotions. When Jesus was in the Garden of Gethsemane just prior to his crucifixion, he cried; **"My soul is exceedingly sorrowful, even unto death"** *(Matthew 26:38)*.

The Body

Most of us have been to a burial service of someone we knew; a loved one or friend or associate. It is therefore easy for us to understand what happens to their body after that. The body is typically buried in the ground or cremated. The Bible says it this way; *Genesis 3:19 In the sweat of thy face shalt thou eat bread, till <u>thou return unto the ground</u>; for out of it wast thou taken: <u>for dust thou art, and unto dust shalt thou return</u>.*

So, the case for the **Body** is easily made from observation (burial or cremation) and from the revelation of the Scriptures. But is that all there is to a life...a little bit of dust?

The Spirit

The Spirit within us is part of the unseen spiritual domain of human beings. What does the Bible say about our unseen spirit? We find the answer to this in the book of *Ecclesiastes 12:7* which address the body and the spirit; *Then shall the <u>dust</u> return to the earth as it was: and <u>the spirit shall return unto God who gave it</u>.* The spirit of a person is said to be the breath of God *(Genesis 2:7)*, and those spirits return to God in some fashion.

The Soul

So far, we have seen the body returning to the dust and the spirit returning to God. What about our soul, what happens to it? According to the Bible your soul has only one of two places where it will end up; Heaven or Hell. We will look at both Heaven and Hell in more detail a bit later, so for now, let's stay on point.

When Jesus was on earth, he spoke of both Heaven and Hell. In the Gospel of John (chapter 14), he called Heaven, his *"Father's house"*. In the Gospel of Luke (chapter 23), he called Heaven *"Paradise"*. The Bible says that when a (born-again) Christian dies they go to Heaven (*2 Corinthians 5:6-8; "absent from the body, and to be present with the Lord"*), awaiting the resurrection of their body in newness of life *(1 Corinthians 15:50-57).*

Jesus also spoke very vividly about a place called Hell, describing it as a place of torments in *Luke 16:23; "And in hell he lift up his eyes, being in torments...".* The way to Hell is through unbelief and in rejecting the Gospel of Jesus Christ.

So, to briefly summarize; the Bible teaches that a person's soul will wind up in Heaven or Hell. There are no other choices given in Scripture. There is no Nirvana, no stages of the soul to walk through, and there is no Purgatory to wait in. And as we all know and will discuss later; **Heaven is good and Hell is bad!**

Heaven is gained by trusting in the Lord Jesus Christ as your Saviour while Hell is found by rejecting him...it's that plain in the Bible. *And they said, Believe on the Lord Jesus Christ, and thou shalt be saved, and thy house. (Acts 16:31)*

Question 4
When I die, will I live again?

What a great question. Another way to ask it is; "Is this life all there is or is there more"? The Scriptures are very open on this subject and as always, God wants us to know the answer for certain. The Patriarch Job (pronounced "Jobe") asked it like this; *"If a man die, shall he live again?* In the case of the man Job, he was confident that he indeed would live again after he died. He said; *For I know that my redeemer liveth, and that he shall stand at the latter day upon the earth: 26 And though after my skin worms destroy this body, yet in my flesh shall I see God: 27 Whom I shall see for myself, and mine eyes shall behold, and not another; though my reins be consumed within me. (Job 19:25-27)*

Somehow Job knew that he would see God one day even though he would face death. According to the Bible, this life you now live is NOT all there is. Let me relate a true story from the Gospel of John about two sisters and a brother. The sister's names were Mary and Martha and the brother was named Lazarus. One day Lazarus died. His sisters were very sorrowful over the loss of their brother as most of us would be if we lost a sibling to death. I know from the death of my older brother what a loss this is and how much it hurts. But the account doesn't end with Lazarus in the grave because Jesus showed up for a visit. Let's pick up the story from this point as told to us through the Scriptures.

Then Martha, as soon as she heard that Jesus was coming, went and met him: but Mary sat still in the house. 21 Then said Martha unto Jesus, Lord, if thou hadst been here, my brother had not died. 22 But I know, that even now, whatsoever thou wilt ask of God, God will give it thee. 23 Jesus saith unto her, Thy brother shall rise again. 24 Martha saith unto him, I know that he shall rise again in the resurrection at the last day. 25 Jesus said unto her, I am the resurrection, and the life: he that believeth in me, though he were dead, yet shall he live: 26 And whosoever liveth and believeth in me shall never die. Believest thou this? 27 She saith unto him, Yea, Lord: I believe that thou art the Christ, the Son of God, which should come into the world. (John 11:20-27)

We learn a lot from these few verses...we learn why the man Job from our previous verses was so confident that even after he died, he would see his Redeemer God.

In the verses from John's Gospel, Jesus reveals something about himself, and life after death. Here it is again; *Jesus said unto her, I am the resurrection, and the life: he that believeth in me, though he were dead, yet shall he live.* Jesus plainly said that believing in him would bring life after death, and therefore a person trusting him would never really die...because Jesus was (himself) the *"resurrection, and the life"*.

There is something else important to learn; the life Jesus was talking about was Everlasting or Eternal life! Eternal life is just that, a promise to live forever. But it won't be life like we have it now; with pain, sorrow, suffering, doubt and loss. No, it is life void of those very things that trouble us in this life we now live. We will look at this in detail later when we discuss Heaven, but right now I want to discuss what is required to inherit this Eternal Life.

Question 5
<u>What Must I Do to Inherit Eternal Life?</u>

And, behold, a certain lawyer stood up, and tempted him, saying, Master, what shall I do to inherit eternal life?

One day a lawyer approached Jesus with a question about the requirements for inheriting Eternal Life. Jesus replied; *"What is written in the law? How readest thou"?* When Jesus referred to the "law" he was speaking about the Scriptures as they were often referred to in that way. But what was Jesus really saying by telling the lawyer to look to the Scriptures (Bible)? The key to this lies in another verse from the Bible; *Search the scriptures; for in them ye think ye have eternal life: and they are they which testify of me.* We turn to the Scriptures because they tell us about Jesus, and Jesus tells us what we must do to inherit Eternal Life.

This is such an important teaching that I want to work carefully through some Bible verses together to clearly show how we may inherit Eternal Life, and know it, like the Patriarch Job did.

Jesus is Eternal Life

Jesus said unto her, I am the resurrection, and the life: he that believeth in me, though he were dead, yet shall he live: 26 And whosoever liveth and believeth in me shall never die. Believest thou this? 27 She saith unto him, Yea, Lord: I believe that thou art the Christ, the Son of God, which should come into the world.

Jesus said in another place; *Jesus saith unto him, I am the way, the truth, and the life: no man cometh unto the Father, but by me.*

Jesus Christ lived a sinless life in full obedience to his Heavenly Father. And because of this, and his faithfulness to fulfill the Father's will, Jesus died on the cross of Calvary to pay for the sins of the whole world. God accepted Jesus' death as a substitute for you and I. This is called "Propitiation" (Payment). The Bible says; *And he is the propitiation for our sins: and not for ours only, but also for the sins of the whole world.*

But how do I inherit this Eternal Life? The simple answer is, by faith. But not just faith in anything or anyone; it is faith in the Lord Jesus Christ and his Gospel. Remember, the Gospel is the Good News that Jesus Christ died, was buried for three days, but rose from death and the grave to offer Eternal Life to those who would put their trust in him fully. This requires a bit more discussion from the Bible because so many of us have been taught we can't know for sure what happens to us when we die, or that we must do something (good works, confession, penance, etc.) to hopefully earn a place in Heaven. This is not what the Bible teaches and so we will look at the plain words of Scripture to see exactly what it does say about inheriting this Eternal Life.

As I stated, faith is the currency to "buy" your eternal salvation; faith in Jesus Christ and his finished work on the cross.

> *For ye are all the children of God by faith in Christ Jesus. (Galatians 3:26)*

We see from this verse that what is required to become a true spiritual child of God is *faith in Christ Jesus.* Read carefully the following words from the Apostle Paul.

> *Romans 10:8 But what saith it? The word is nigh thee, even in thy mouth, and in thy heart: that is, <u>the word of faith</u>, which we preach; 9 That if thou shalt <u>confess with thy mouth the Lord Jesus</u>, and shalt <u>believe in thine heart that God hath raised him from the dead, thou shalt be saved</u>. 10 For with the heart man believeth unto righteousness; and with the mouth confession is made unto salvation. 11 For the scripture saith, Whosoever believeth on him shall not be ashamed. 12 For there is no difference between the Jew and the Greek: for the same Lord over all is rich unto all that call upon him. 13*

***For whosoever shall call upon the name of the Lord shall be
saved.***

    I know there is a lot there so please read it carefully and ask God
to give you understanding. You may not understand everything right
now, but if you do what the verse says; (1) Confess with your mouth
the Lord Jesus and (2) believe in your heart his Gospel and (3) call on
the name of the Lord Jesus Christ **you will be saved!** In the Book of the
Acts of the Apostles, we find it even more simply stated; *"Believe on
the Lord Jesus Christ, and thou shalt be saved"*. While the choice to
believe or not is totally yours, it is the only prescribed way given by
God to receive everlasting life.

Salvation is Not of Good Works

    Many of us grew up in a religious tradition that taught that we
must do good works to eventually earn our way to Heaven. But the
Scripture tells another story. Look at these three verses from the letter
of St. Paul the Apostle to the Ephesian church. I will break it down one
verse at a time.

> ***Ephesians 2:8 For by grace are ye saved through faith; and
> that not of yourselves: it is the gift of God:***

    In verse 8 above we see once again that it is faith that is required
for salvation. Notice also, salvation is a gift God bestows by his grace
(favor) to anyone who believes by faith.

> ***Ephesians 2:9 Not of works, lest any man should boast.***

    We see here in verse 9 very explicitly that (good) works of any sort,
or any amount, cannot earn us a spot in Heaven. This is the very reason
Jesus died on the cross; to take away the sins of the world.

> ***Ephesians 2:10 For we are his workmanship, created in Christ
> Jesus unto good works, which God hath before ordained that
> we should walk in them.***

Now <u>after salvation by faith</u>, works enter into the picture. You see, works don't save you but they are expected of you by God. And these very works, done in the name of Jesus, testify to the fact that God has done his work of salvation in your heart already.

You Can Know Now That You Are Saved

Growing up I was taught that you could not know for sure whether or not you would be going to Heaven when you die. But once again we find that the Bible is very clear on this issue. Let's take a look.

> *1 John 5: 11 And this is the record, that <u>God</u> hath <u>given</u> to us <u>eternal life</u>, and this <u>life is in his Son</u>. 12 He that hath the Son hath life; and he that hath not the Son of God hath not life. 13 These things have I written unto you that believe on the name of the Son of God; that ye may <u>know</u> that ye have eternal life, and that ye may believe on the name of the Son of God.*

I underlined a few important points from these verses, but the truth is, all of the verses are important. Look at what it clearly says:
1. God gave the gift of eternal life
2. This gift is in Jesus Christ alone
3. If you trust Jesus by faith, you have eternal life
4. If you do not trust Jesus by faith, you do not have eternal life
5. You can know whether or not you have eternal life now
6. Believe on the name of the Son of God; his name is Jesus!

Chapter 3
The Issues of Life; More Questions for God

Question 1
Why Do People Suffer and Die?

It is a sad thing indeed that there is great suffering in this life, and that death is certain. I have lived long enough to see both great suffering and all too frequent death. But this was never God's desire or intent, and this is not the way it was in the beginning. God created Adam and Eve to live forever and to walk in fellowship with him. God also created Adam and Eve with a free will to choose whether or not they would obey him. Unfortunately, when a test of their obedience arrived in the form of a temping Serpent (Satan), Eve was beguiled into disobedience and Adam soon followed after her.

This is a true story of the first man and woman and Jesus himself testified to its authenticity when he was here on earth. Referring to Adam and Eve, he said; *Have ye not read, that he which made them at the beginning made them male and female?* When Adam knowingly fell into sin a whole new and unfortunate number of words were added to his vocabulary. He would now learn **fear**, **suffering**, **toil** and **death**. These were words I am sure God never intended for his Creation to learn.

God had clearly warned Adam of the dire consequences of any disobedience to his word. He said; *(Genesis 2:15) And the LORD God took the man, and put him into the garden of Eden to dress it and to keep it. 16 And the LORD God commanded the man, saying, Of every tree of the garden thou mayest freely eat: 17 But of the tree of the knowledge of good and evil, thou shalt not eat of it: for in the day that thou eatest thereof thou shalt surely die.*

So here is the sad reality; the disobedience (SIN) of Adam brought trials, tribulations and eventually death into this world. We read in *1*

Corinthians 15:21-22 the following words; *For since by man came death, by man came also the resurrection of the dead. :22 For as in Adam all die, even so in Christ shall all be made alive.*

This is the reason God came to earth in human form (Jesus Christ). He came to pay the price that God demanded for sin. The price would be the blood of his beloved Son. As it turns out, this blood is said to be *"God's blood"* in the Book of Acts 20:28. God so loved you and me that he gave himself for us! What a God, what a Saviour! When no one else was able to step forward and pay the price of sin, Jesus willingly did that for each one of us. And look at the wonderful end to the story of sin in the following verses of Scripture:

> *Romans 6:23 For the wages of sin is death; <u>BUT</u> the gift of God is eternal life through Jesus Christ our Lord.*
>
> *1Corinthians 15:55 O death, where is thy sting? O grave, where is thy victory? 56 The sting of death is sin; and the strength of sin is the law. 57 But thanks be to God, which giveth us the victory through our Lord Jesus Christ.*

Don't miss out on eternal life; by faith turn your heart toward the Lord Jesus Christ. You will find that he has already turned his toward you.

Question 2
Will God Forgive Me?

Sometimes people have done such terrible things in their life and doubt whether or not God will forgive them. I can assure you God can and will forgive you of any sin that has been confessed to him by faith. According to the Bible, he will cleanse you of the penalty and guilt of your sin.

> *1Jn 1:8 If we say that we have no sin, we deceive ourselves, and the truth is not in us. 9 If we confess our sins, he is faithful and just to forgive us our sins, and to cleanse us from all unrighteousness. 10 If we say that we have not sinned, we make him a liar, and his word is not in us.*

The reality is that we are all sinners to one extent or another. The Bible makes that abundantly clear and our own hearts confirm it. The good news is that Jesus died to save sinners...that was the whole point of his sacrifice. Here are two examples, one from the Old Testament and one from the New Testament of two men who sinned greatly but were forgiven for their sin when they confessed it to God and asked for forgiveness.

In the Old Testament of the Bible, we read of King David of Israel. He was chosen by God to lead the people of Israel and did so for 40 years. We read further of David's great sin in the murder of a man under his authority named Uriah. David took Uriah's wife and she became pregnant. In order to cover up his sin he had Uriah killed and then married his wife, Bath-sheba. You can read the full account in 2 Samuel 11 for all the sorted details. When David eventually asked God for forgiveness, God forgave him and continued to bless him. It is important to point out that while God forgave him of his sin, his sin would have grave consequences later in his life with his children. You see, every sin has its own weight of consequence...even if forgiven. But unconfessed and unforgiven sin has even greater consequences.

In the New Testament we read of a man named Saul (later named Paul, the Apostle). Paul was a great religious man, but he hated everything that had to do with Jesus. He persecuted the early church and even assented to the death of a man named Stephen. Later, upon the confession of his sins and the acknowledging of Jesus Christ as his Saviour, Paul became a great Apostle of the Lord and was used mightily to spread the Gospel of Jesus Christ wherever he went.

So you see, your sin no matter what it is can be forgiven by God and you can be cleansed from that sin. There is no sin so great that Calvary's love did not already pay the price for it. Remember, God the Father required a payment for sins and Jesus made that payment in full when he died on the cross of Calvary. Come to him by faith and receive that forgiveness.

Question 3
Did God Create Evil in the World?

One look at any news report on TV, Newspaper or Radio on any given day in our country or around the world, and you know evil exits. There are thefts, lies, fraud and murder everywhere you look. Did God create evil? The answer is yes...and most importantly, NO. Let me explain.

I form the light, and create darkness: I make peace, and create evil: I the LORD do all these things. (Isiah 45:7)

There are two distinct meanings of the word "evil". The first has to do with the wickedness of the world; the murders and thefts that I mentioned. God did not create this as I will discuss in a moment. The other definition of evil has to do with the sorrow that God will bring upon evil doers as part of their judgment. So, in this case, evil is the punishment God will bring upon the evil wicked. This is the evil he created...future judgment on the wicked.

As to the evil (wickedness) we see in the world, this is the result of the fall into sin of Adam, and our own sin which we commit. It is the result of a spiritually darkened heart.

> *For out of the heart proceed evil thoughts, murders, adulteries, fornications, thefts, false witness, blasphemies: (Matthew 15:19)*

> *The heart is deceitful above all things, and desperately wicked: who can know it? (Jerimiah 17:9)*

This is why each and every one of us needs a spiritual heart transplant. We need the Lord to give us a clean heart through faith. This is something only He can truly do. Pray as the Psalmist did...

> *Create in me a clean heart, O God; and renew a right spirit within me. (Psalm 51:10)*

Question 4
Why Should I Pray?

Prayer is talking to God in our spirit. We may pray aloud or silently; it doesn't matter to God. Prayer could be public or in secret, depending on the circumstance or situation. There are many books written exclusively on the subject of prayer and they dive deeper into this subject but let me at this point offer the most important advice about prayer I can give you...Just do it...pray!

God does hear and answer prayer. Sometimes God answers "yes", sometimes "no" and sometimes "be patient". And yet, there is great encouragement throughout the Bible to pray. Here are just a few examples of that encouragement:

> *1Timothy 2:8 I will therefore that men pray every where, lifting up holy hands, without wrath and doubting.*

1Thessaloaians 5:17 Pray without ceasing.

Matthew 26:41 Watch and pray, that ye enter not into temptation: the spirit indeed is willing, but the flesh is weak.

I offer one final example of the encouragement of God to seek him in prayer for strength and help.

Hebrews 4:16 Let us therefore come boldly unto the throne of grace, that we may obtain mercy, and find grace to help in time of need.

It is important to distinguish certain aspects of prayer that are highlighted in the Scriptures.

The Prayer for salvation:

When a person cries out to God by faith and in true repentance of heart, God will hear and answer that prayer with a resounding, "Yes". Remember, Jesus came, died and rose again to save people from the penalty of their sins, so of course he will answer this prayer. Here is one such example of this from the Bible.

Romans 10:9 That if thou shalt confess with thy mouth the Lord Jesus, and shalt believe in thine heart that God hath raised him from the dead, thou shalt be saved. 10 For with the heart man believeth unto righteousness; and with the mouth confession Is made unto salvation. 11 For the scripture saith, Whosoever believeth on him shall not be ashamed. 12 For there is no difference between the Jew and the Greek: for the same Lord over all is rich unto all that call upon him. 13 <u>For whosoever shall call upon the name of the Lord shall be saved</u>.

You can confidently call on the Lord for salvation anytime and anywhere and know he will hear and gladly answer you…" Yes".

The Prayer of Intercession:

There are times that we pray on behalf of someone else. That person may be spiritually lost or ill or dying. The encouragement still is to pray, but the answer sadly is not always a yes answer. King David was a man beloved of God. God chose him as King over the Nation of Israel and blessed him with victories over his enemies during times of war. God allowed David to write much of the Psalms of the Bible, even calling David the "sweet Psalmist of Israel". And yet, there was a time when David prayed to the Lord to spare his newborn child and the Lord did not do so. In that case it was because of David's sin of adultery with another man's wife. Yet, we still see in David the right attitude toward prayer in the midst of not knowing how God would answer. Here is what David said; *And he said, While the child was yet alive, I fasted and wept: for I said, Who can tell whether GOD will be gracious to me, that the child may live? (2 Samuel 12:22)*

When God does not give us the desires of our heart by answering our prayer like we want, he will give you peace.

> *Philippians 4:6 Be careful for nothing; but in every thing by prayer and supplication with thanksgiving let your requests be made known unto God. 7 And the peace of God, which passeth all understanding, shall keep your hearts and minds through Christ Jesus.*

It is at these times we come to trust him more...when the answer does not seem to come, he will keep your heart and mind with his matchless peace.

The Prayer for Self:

The Apostle Paul was a great man of God. He was allowed to write most of the New Testament books of the Bible and was a great Missionary, preaching the Gospel where ever he went. Paul had a great need in his life; there was some trouble that he could not overcome. It appears from Scripture that it was a physical ailment of some kind. He asked God in prayer to remove this from his life. Here is the account of his prayer and God's answer.

> **2Corinthians 12:7 And lest I should be exalted above measure through the abundance of the revelations, there was given to me a thorn in the flesh, the messenger of Satan to buffet me, lest I should be exalted above measure. 8 For this thing I besought the Lord thrice, that it might depart from me. 9 And he said unto me, My grace is sufficient for thee: for my strength is made perfect in weakness. Most gladly therefore will I rather glory in my infirmities, that the power of Christ may rest upon me.**

So, when God's answer is "no", he will give you his grace to get you through and make you strong in your weakness.

The Prayer of Spiritual Battle:

There are times we battle for the souls of a loved one and we need the resource of prayer. When we are in such a battle the Bible teaches that we are actually wrestling against *"principalities, against powers, against the rulers of the darkness of this world, against spiritual wickedness in high places". (Ephesians 6:12)* As such, we need a spiritual weapon...and prayer is that weapon...never forget or underestimate prayer in this battle.

There are other times when we are the one under some kind of spiritual attack from the enemy of our soul, Satan. This is when we need to pray the most; for strength, for grace and for wisdom and deliverance. Ask the Lord to remove the spiritual threat and to give you the ability to resist the Devil by faith.

The Prayer of Thanksgiving:

> *Psalm 69:30 I will praise the name of God with a song, and will magnify him with thanksgiving.*

It is good to give God thanks for his blessings and provisions in your life. Like any good parent, God loves to hear his children praise him and thank him…so don't leave off this aspect of prayer from your life. When you do thank him, you will find your heart rejoicing in God your Saviour, and that's a good thing all around.

Question 5
Where is God When I Need Him Most?

Many have asked this question over the centuries. The answer can be found in the Bible. But it is also found in the lives of some of God's faithful servants, and so, we will look at both.

Here are just a few of the Bible verses that tell us just where God is when we need him the most. They are great and precious verses that tell us something of God's character and desire for those that love and trust him. Read carefully and draw on their wisdom and strength.

The Testimony of Scripture:

> *God is our refuge and strength, a very present help in trouble. (Psalm 46:1)*

> *He only is my rock and my salvation: he is my defence; I shall not be moved. 7 In God is my salvation and my glory: the rock of my strength, and my refuge, is in God. 8 Trust in him at all times; ye people, pour out your heart before him: God is a refuge for us. Selah. (Psalm 62:6-8)*

Let your conversation be without covetousness; and be content with such things as ye have: for he hath said, I will never leave thee, nor forsake thee. (Hebrews 13:5)

The Testimony of God's People:

There are many servants of God both in the Scriptures and outside of the Scriptures who can attest to God's help and presence when needed most. It was king David who penned the words above from the Psalms, and it was the apostle Paul who wrote that the Lord would *"never leave thee nor forsake thee".* But there are many other of God's children who can say Amen to Paul's claim.

Corrie Ten Boom – Corrie and her family lived in the Netherlands during the Second World War. Her family risked their own lives hiding the Jews from the Nazis in a secret hiding place in their home. All worked well until they were betrayed by a neighbor who found out their secret. As a result, her family was captured and taken to Nazi Concentration Camps. The men were separated from the women in different camps. While in prison, Corrie's father, brother and sister died. She herself suffered many atrocities at the hands of the Nazis. Corrie was eventually released from prison due to a "clerical error" on the part of the Germans. Eventually she went on to write numerous books and travelled the world with her message of God's faithfulness and help. Many times, during her imprisonment God would comfort her and provide her the hope she needed...God had not forsaken her, and was indeed there with her all the time she was in Nazi hands.

Haralan Popov - At 4 a.m. on July 24, 1948, Dr. Haralan Popov, a prominent pastor, was arrested by the Bulgarian Secret Police on false charges of "being a spy" for the United States and Great Britain. After intense torture and brainwashing, Haralan confessed to being a "spy", though he wasn't.

He spent the next 13 years in 16 communist prisons and concentration camps for his uncompromising faith in Jesus

Christ. Despite tremendous suffering and torture, he continued his work for God inside the prison to reach fellow prisoners.

After his release from prison in 1961, he was eventually reunited with his family in 1963. He immediately began telling the world of the plight of persecuted Christians and began to bring God's Word into communist countries where Bibles had been confiscated and burned.

God had walked through trials with him and sustained him through it all.

Question 6
Will God Heal Me or My Loved One?

What a powerful question. This is a question that often comes from the deepest part of a hurting heart. Let's take a look at what the Bible has to say about healing.

When Jesus was here on earth, he healed many people of their diseases. The purpose was to demonstrate and prove to others that he indeed was the Messiah sent from Heaven to save people from their sin. Later, he would pass this power to his Apostles as further evidence that the Messiah had indeed come. After the death of the Apostles and the completion of the Holy Scriptures, this ministry of healing appears to have largely disappeared. I know that there are people you see on T.V. who promise you healing, but this is a promise they are not qualified to make.

There is a prophecy of Jesus' death in the Old Testament book of the Prophet Isaiah. It says; **"But he was wounded for our transgressions, he was bruised for our iniquities: the chastisement of our peace was upon him; and with his stripes we are healed"**. The Prophet said that Jesus took the judgment of God upon himself and provided healing to people. This verse is telling us that Jesus' death and resurrection provides healing...spiritual healing now...and physical healing when we are with him in Heaven.

In Heaven, not earth, we find the blessing of physical healing for everyone. Here is what the Bible tells us about life in Heaven with respect to healing the physical struggles we all face.

> *Revelation 21:4 And God shall wipe away all tears from their eyes; and there shall be no more death, neither sorrow, nor crying, neither shall there be any more pain: for the former things are passed away.*

So, the Biblical truth is that physical healing now is not a guarantee. If you have a sick loved one, I would recommend praying for them. It may be that God through prayer will heal them physically now. But when the physical healing does not come now there is God's grace to see us through until the other side. You see, part of being a Christian is suffering with Christ now. The Bible says it like this; *"That I may know him, and the power of his resurrection, and the fellowship of his sufferings, being made conformable unto his death;" (Philippians 3:10).* It is this very process of being conformed to Christ in his sufferings that is troublesome for us now. But in the end, the Bible promises that it will be worth it because eternity is much more important than our 70 or 80 years now.

> *For our light affliction, which is but for a moment, worketh for us a far more exceeding and eternal weight of glory; (2 Corinthians 4:17)*

Question 7
Is Heaven Real?

I have written this book as if Heaven is a real place, which it is. When Jesus was here on earth, he told his disciples that he was going to his Father's house (Heaven) to prepare a **place** for them. Let's take some time talking a little bit about Heaven.

One day the Apostle Paul was stoned to death by *"certain Jews from Antioch and Iconium".* In his spirit, he was taken up into Heaven for a short period of time. Some people like to think of it as a "near-death experience" but in this case we know that Paul's account is real. When he returned to his body, and then some years later, he said that if he had to die and return to Heaven, it would be far better than remaining here on earth *(Philippians 1:21-23)*. Here was a man who got a glimpse of Heaven and did not want to stay any longer on earth. His desire was to depart earth and return to Heaven. This gives us a general sense that whatever Heaven is like, it is to be preferred to life on earth!

What is it about Heaven that was so attractive for Paul? Afterall, he would have to die to get there. Didn't he fear dying? Apparently not! Because he knew what awaited him on the other side.

Let's examine some of the verses concerning Heaven.

1. It is a real place with many mansions in it *(John 14:1)*
2. It is a place of everlasting life *(1 John 5:11-13)*
3. It is a place of everlasting joy and pleasure *(Psalm 16:11)*
4. It is a place where we will no longer need doctors because there will be no more death and disease *(Revelation 21:4)*
5. It is a place where all doubts and regrets of this life will completely and for ever disappear. *(Revelation 21:4)*
6. It is a place that Jesus called; Paradise *(Luke 23:43)*
7. It is a place of singing and worship *(Revelation 5:8-9)*

The best part of Heaven is the fact that God is there; the Father, the Son and the Holy Ghost.

> *Revelation 22:1 And he shewed me a pure river of water of life, clear as crystal, proceeding out of the throne of God and of the Lamb. 2 In the midst of the street of it, and on either side of the river, was there the tree of life, which bare twelve manner of fruits, and yielded her fruit every month: and the leaves of the tree were for the healing of the nations. 3 And there shall be no more curse: but the throne of God and of the Lamb shall be in it; and his servants shall serve him:*

This is the place where you will finally be home and at eternal peace. No one will ever come around to evict you. There is no mortgage that needs to be paid by you. You will be home; in perfect love and acceptance.

In order to be able to call Heaven your home you must put in a reservation ahead of time. *1 Peter 1:3 Blessed be the God and Father of our Lord Jesus Christ, which according to his abundant mercy hath begotten us again unto a lively hope by the <u>resurrection of Jesus Christ</u> from the dead, 4 To an <u>inheritance</u> incorruptible, and undefiled, and that fadeth not away, <u>reserved in heaven for you</u>,*

The only way to assure your reservation is complete is to put your trust in the Lord Jesus Christ. The bible says of him; *Acts 4:12 Neither is there salvation in any other: for there is none other name under heaven given among men, whereby we must be saved.*

Don't delay; yesterday is past and tomorrow may not come for you. All you have of time to spend, is Now. The Bible says; *behold, now is the accepted time; behold, now is the day of salvation.)*

Question 8
Is Hell Real?

As the blessing of Heaven is real, so too is the terror of Hell. Let me point out right away that Hell was not created for mankind, but for the Devil and his angels. *Matthew 25:41 Then shall he say also unto them on the left hand, Depart from me, ye cursed, into everlasting fire, prepared for the devil and his angels:*

There are many notions about Hell. But since Hell is unseen by us today, we must rely on the knowledge of God, who created it. Hell is the place where those who reject the death, burial and resurrection of Jesus Christ will find themselves. Jesus warned about Hell because he knew it was real and he did not want anyone to go there...this is why he died on the cross of Calvary 2000 years ago, to pay for the sins of people and to keep people out of Hell.

Hell is spoken of in Scripture in very specific terms, and none of it is good. Take these few verses for instance:

> *2Samuel 22:6 The <u>sorrows of hell</u> compassed me about; the snares of death prevented me;*

> *Psalm 116:3 The sorrows of death compassed me, and the <u>pains of hell</u> gat hold upon me: I found trouble and sorrow.*

> *Matthew 5:22 ... Thou fool, shall be in danger of <u>hell fire</u>.*

> *Matthew 23:33 Ye serpents, ye generation of vipers, how can ye escape the <u>damnation of hell</u>?*

> *Luke 16:23 And in <u>hell</u> he lift up his eyes, being in <u>torments</u>, and seeth Abraham afar off, and Lazarus in his bosom.*

The good news is that no one needs to ever spend one minute in Hell. There is one who has conquered death *(1 Corinthians 15:54-58)* and has the keys of Hell and death; his name is Jesus Christ, the only begotten Son of the Father. There is no a way out of Hell, but there is a way to avoid it altogether; by faith in Jesus Christ. Won't you ask Jesus right now to save your soul and give you everlasting life? The Bible says; *"Believe on the Lord Jesus Christ, and thou shalt be saved…".*

> *Revelation 1:18 I am he that liveth, and was dead; and, behold, I am alive for evermore, Amen; and have the keys of hell and of death.*

> *Proverbs 15:24 The way of life is above to the wise, that he may depart from hell beneath.*

Question 9
Isn't it Enough if I keep the 10 Commandment?

This is a great question. God gave the 10 Commandments for us to obey. If I obey them won't that be good enough to earn a place in Heaven? The short answer is, NO. But we need to explore this further.

God gave Israel 10 Commandments in the Old Testament when he was establishing their Nation. Here they are in brief format from Exodus 20:

1. Thou shalt have no other gods before me.
2. Thou shalt not make unto thee any graven image (statue or idol)
3. Thou shalt not take the name of the LORD thy God in vain.
4. Remember the sabbath day, to keep it holy.
5. Honour thy father and thy mother.
6. Thou shalt not kill.
7. Thou shalt not commit adultery.
8. Thou shalt not steal.
9. Thou shalt not bear false witness against thy neighbor.
10. Thou shalt not covet thy neighbor's possessions or his wife.

That is God's perfect list of the moral code of conduct between man and God, and between man and humanity. The Commandments were given to the Nation of Israel and then passed down through time to the rest of humanity. It was God's way of setting the standard of conduct for his Creation. It would assist mankind in fellowship both with God and with his fellow man. These Commandments are part of what the Bible refers to as "The Law" of God.

There is no problem with the Law; *"Psalm 19:7 The law of the LORD is perfect"*. The problem is not with the Commandments (The Law), but with our inability to obey it 100% of the time, every day of our lives!

Watch carefully what the Bible says about the Commandment's ability to save a person.

> *Hebrews 7:19 For the law made nothing perfect, but the bringing in of a better hope did; by the which we draw nigh unto God.*

> *Hebrews 10:1 For the law having a shadow of good things to come, and not the very image of the things, can never with those sacrifices which they offered year by year continually make the comers thereunto perfect.*

The two verses above from the book of Hebrews make it perfectly clear that the law (Commandments) did not make anyone perfect before God. The Law (Commandments) hinted at something better, some better hope of eternal life. The only weakness of the Law (Commandments) is me...I can't keep them perfectly and so am guilty before God of breaking his Commandments. The Bible makes this abundantly clear when it states; *"for by the works of the law (Commandments) shall no flesh be justified".*

What then was the purpose of the 10 Commandments if I can't keep them all and they won't earn me a place in Heaven with God? The Scriptures tells us explicitly:

> *Galatians 3:24 Wherefore the law was our schoolmaster to bring us unto Christ, that we might be justified by faith. 25 But after that faith is come, we are no longer under a schoolmaster. 26 For ye are all the children of God by faith in Christ Jesus.*

God gave the Commandments for an earthly purpose and a Heavenly purpose. The earthly purpose was to show mankind the right way to live. The Heavenly purpose was to show mankind that no matter how good a person is, they could never earn Heaven. Further, the law (Commandments) was a way for God to point to the only one who could lead us into Heaven; the Lord Jesus Christ. The law became our school teacher to teach us about faith because as it goes on to say, faith is the key ingredient for the salvation of your soul, not good works.

There is another passage of Scripture that further explains this relationship between faith, good works and salvation. The Apostle Paul was writing to the church at Ephesus around A.D. 64. In his letter he wrote these words given to him by God:

> **Ephesians 2:8 For by grace are ye saved through faith; and that not of yourselves: it is the gift of God: 9 Not of works, lest any man should boast. 10 For we are his workmanship, created in Christ Jesus unto good works, which God hath before ordained that we should walk in them.**

Verse 8 above tells us that it is by God's grace (unmerited favor) through our faith in Him that saves us. Verse 9 tells us that this salvation is a free gift, not an earned reward! Verse 10 goes on to explain that once we are saved by God's grace through faith, we should do good and obey his Commandments...but it is NOT this "doing good" that earns a place in Heaven with God.

Question 10
What about forgiving others?

Here is a question that speaks directly to a person's heart and inner needs. Everyone has had to face this question at some point. Everyone has been hurt by someone (and likely you have hurt someone). Let's begin to examine this very important and often delicate question from the Bible. I want to tread carefully here as we look for direction and help from the Scriptures. I understand that some people have been hurt very, very badly by others.

Forgiveness is not an excuse for a person to simply allow another to abuse them. If there is real abuse going on in a relationship the abused must take appropriate action to alleviate the abuse of whatever sort it is and be safe.

I want to start off by an example that Jesus gave us in his own life when he was here on earth. Jesus was crucified on a cross at Calvary for the sins of the world. While he was hanging there dying, he spoke briefly several times. The first of these sayings went like this; *"Father, forgive them; for they know not what they do"*. While dying at the hands of the people, he asked the Father to forgive them. I believe very strongly that this implies that Jesus had forgiven them already. As a matter of fact, Jesus came and was crucified to offer eternal forgiveness to all who would come to Him by faith.

There was another time that Jesus' disciples asked him about the question of forgiving others. In this interaction (below) with the Apostle Peter, Jesus emphasizes the need to seek forgiveness in your own heart for the hurt done to you by others.

> *Matthew 18:21 Then came Peter to him, and said, Lord, how oft shall my brother sin against me, and I forgive him? till seven times? 22 Jesus saith unto him, I say not unto thee, Until seven times: but, Until seventy times seven.*

Forgiveness is a process and can often be painful emotionally. When we seek to forgive in our own heart it does not mean the other party is guiltless of the hurt they have caused you; they will still answer to Almighty God for their own deeds. And we will have to answer for the forgiveness we give or withhold.

I want to tell you a true story that took place during World War II about a woman commonly known as Corrie ten Boom. Corrie was born, Cornelia ten Boom in April 1892. She was a Dutch watchmaker who later became a Christian writer and public witness for the Lord Jesus Christ. She and her family worked diligently to help many Jewish people escape from the Nazis during the Holocaust in World War II by hiding them in her home. There is an excellent movie documenting the events called, The Hiding Place. They were caught by the Nazis, and she was arrested and sent to the Ravensbrück concentration camp with her sister. Her other family members were arrested, sent to other camps, and eventually died in those camps. A few years later, Corrie was released from Ravensbrück due to a "clerical error". Still years later, she became a travelling speaker for her Saviour, Jesus Christ. Corrie recounts, one evening after one particular speech, that she saw in the receiving line an ex-prison guard from Ravensbrück who was standing in line to introduce himself. As you well imagine, Corrie was horrified to think that this once brutal guard would want to shake her hand. As he got closer to her, she said to herself; "I can't forgive this man for his mistreatment to me and my sister, Lord, please help me". As the man approached and held out his hand she felt as thou the Lord had taken over the situation in a miraculous way and she reached her hand out and greeted him, as God's forgiveness flooded her soul. This is something only the Lord Jesus can do...but we must ask him to help.

Even those closest to Jesus had trouble understanding and applying this. Take a look at another account in the Gospel of Luke that Jesus had with some of his disciples on this very subject.

Luke 17:3 Take heed to yourselves: If thy brother trespass against thee, rebuke him; and if he repent, forgive him. :4

And if he trespass against thee seven times in a day, and seven times in a day turn again to thee, saying, I repent; thou shalt forgive him. And the apostles said unto the Lord, Increase our faith.

Again, Jesus is trying to emphasize the need to seek forgiveness in your heart toward others who have wronged you in some way. The apostles got it just right when they asked Jesus to increase their faith on this particular matter. Jesus never said it would be easy to forgive, but he did stress that it was important. And Jesus was the great example of forgiveness when he cried out on the cross; *"Father, forgive them…"*.

Let's discuss this important topic a little further from the Bible. If you look at the Bible you will find the word "forgive", or some form of it, over 100 times.

Unforgiveness is a tool of the Devil that he uses to divide and destroy people's lives. The Bible says that he uses it to try to get an advantage over us *(2 Corinthians 2:11)*. If left unchecked in your life, it will cause a deep root of bitterness to grow. Unforgiveness can rob you of your joy and even your health.

Sometimes the person we find it hardest to forgive is ourselves. We have committed some sin we think the Lord won't forgive and we refuse to accept the forgiveness he offers. When Jesus was dying on the cross, he prayed for those around him and asked his Heavenly Father to forgive them of what they were doing to him. And the Father did forgive them as evidenced by the fact that he did not strike the offenders dead for crucifying his Son on the cross. The Lord does not want you to live with unforgiveness for others or yourself. He does not want you to live with the burden of self-placed guilt. You may indeed be guilty of some great sin, but the Bible says that *"where sin did abound, grace did much more abound"*.

When you learn to trust the Lord for forgiveness for yourself or others, you will often see relationships restored, joy returned and true healing begin. Don't let Satan turn unforgiveness in your heart into a weapon he can use to destroy you and destroy those you love the most.

Question 11
What is truth?

This question comes to us from Pontius Pilate in *John 18:38*. Jesus was standing before this Roman procurator of Judea falsely accused of crimes by the Jewish leaders. It was Pilate's job to pronounce judgment. While questioning Jesus, Pilate asked the following question of Jesus; *"What is truth"?*

This is such an important question on the minds of people that many books have been written on the subject. People want to know, is truth absolute or relative? Can two opposing "facts" be true at the same time? Is my truth the same as yours...or is that really just my opinion?

Truth is the opposite of falsehood. Truth is that which describes facts and reality. Truth is therefore understood to be absolute. But where can a person find absolute truth and what is the significance of that?

Truth is so important, and made even more so, by the subject we are discussing. For instance, if you go to your doctor for a checkup and they discover cancer in the early stage of the disease, you don't want your doctor to lie and tell you everything is fine. This brings up another point; truth is not always easy or pleasant to hear. If your son or daughter is killed while in the armed forces you will not want to hear the truth...but it is absolutely necessary that you do.

The Bible has the answer to the question; What is truth? One day Jesus was speaking to his disciples in John 16 and told them that they would face very difficult times because of their belief in him and God the Father. Listen to what the Lord Jesus told them that day:

> *John 16:6 But because I have said these things unto you,*
> *sorrow hath filled your heart. 7 Nevertheless I tell you the*
> *truth;*

Jesus told them the hard truth that day. But he also said that he would always tell them the truth, no matter what.

Let's answer the question now from the Bible...what is truth? Truth is found in the Lord Jesus Christ and his Holy Bible.

> *John 14:6 Jesus saith unto him, I am the way, <u>the truth</u>, and*
> *the life: no man cometh unto the Father, but by me.*

> *John 17:17 Sanctify them through thy truth: <u>thy word is</u>*
> *<u>truth</u>.*

Truth can be defined by looking to Jesus and his Holy Bible. Everything he ever said while on earth or recorded for us in his Bible, is truth...absolute truth. There are no shadows or shades of truth, but truth itself.

Sometimes we don't want to hear the truth for various reasons. Listen to what Jesus said when confronting the hypocritical religious leaders of his day.

> *John 8:45 And because I tell you the truth, ye believe me not.*

The apostle Paul ran into this same issue when he had to address the Galatian believers to inform them that they were getting off on the wrong tract.

> *Galatians 4:16 Am I therefore become your enemy, because I*
> *tell you the truth?*

Truth that is difficult to hear for one reason or another is still truth, and is still necessary. Jesus tells us of the blessing of Heaven with his Father, but he also warns us of the torments of Hell. He does this because he loves those he created. His love could only be measured by his willingness to die on the cross of Calvary. That love which held him on the cross two thousand years ago is still available to anyone who would call upon his name by faith today. *"And they said, Believe on the Lord Jesus Christ, and thou shalt be saved...".*

Question 12
What about the people who have never heard?

A common question that is often put to Christian believers is; what about all the people who have never heard of Jesus? Is God going to punish them? If asked with the right heart attitude, this is a fair question and one that deserves an answer from Holy Scriptures. We learn from Scripture that God has revealed himself to mankind through (1) Creation, (2) Conscience, and (3) the Cross. After looking at each of these in brief, I will answer the question posed above.

Creation -
God the Father made it his business to see to it that every person ever born had an opportunity to know that he exists *(John 1:9)*. In the book of Romans, we learn in chapter one that God had revealed himself to mankind through Creation, and therefore mankind has no excuse in pretending that God does not exist. *Romans 1:20 For the invisible things of him from the creation of the world are clearly seen, being understood by the things that are made, even his eternal power and Godhead; so that they are without excuse:.* The book of the Psalms says; *Psalm 19:1 To the chief Musician, A Psalm of David. The heavens declare the glory of God; and the firmament sheweth his handywork.*

It doesn't require a lot of faith to understand that the vastness of space, with all of its heavenly bodies, and the intricacies of the human body had a Designer and Creator. Faith comes in when you consider Jesus himself; was he God in the flesh or just a man?

Conscience –

God also gave mankind a conscience by which he could reveal to mankind truth. The Bible says that God's truth (the law) was written in their hearts and that mankind's conscience bears witness to the truth of God.

> **Romans 2:15 Which shew the work of the law written in their hearts, their conscience also bearing witness, and their thoughts the mean while accusing or else excusing one another;)**

The Cross –

The greatest revelation that God has given of himself to mankind was the birth, death and resurrection of Jesus Christ. Jesus was God in the flesh in the form of the Son of God. The events of human history are often referred to as B.C. (before Christ) and A.D. (in the year of our Lord). There is no escaping the reality of Jesus Christ. So many accounts have been given in the Bible and outside of the Bible attesting to his reality.

The answer -

The best way to answer this question is to realize that God is just and will only hold somebody accountable based on the level of "light" (revelation of the truth) that a person has received to respond to. If all a person truly has is Creation or Conscience as a witness of God, then God will either hold them accountable to that revelation or reveal more to them in some manner. But those who have heard the gospel or have had the opportunity to do so, are accountable to this full revelation of God. Remember, God is just and will make all his judgments properly *(Genesis 18:25 and Romans 2:5)*.

Chapter 4
The Issues of Life; Questions From God

In this chapter we will explore several questions that God asks of us. If he asks us these questions, you can be sure they are important. Unlike us when we ask him a question, he already knows the answers to his questions. He asks them to get us to consider the answers carefully and to hopefully get us to respond by faith.

Question 1
Why will you die?

Ezekiel 33:11 Say unto them, As I live, saith the Lord GOD, I have no pleasure in the death of the wicked; but that the wicked turn from his way and live: turn ye, turn ye from your evil ways; <u>for why will ye die</u>, O house of Israel?

God had a special relationship with the Nation of Israel for it would be from this Nation that he would bring forth his Son, the Messiah. When speaking to them through the prophet Ezekiel God says some very important words and then asks them a vitally important question; *"why will ye die"?* The Lord had many times spoken to Israel about turning from their wicked ways and returning to a right relationship with him. By asking this question he is trying to get them to consider their ways and choose life.

The same thing can be said to people throughout history, including today. When Jesus died on the cross and rose from the dead he was saying to humanity; *why will ye die?* You don't have to die; this is the Good News of the Gospel. Listen to what Jesus told one of his followers named Martha when her brother Lazarus died.

John 11:25 Jesus said unto her, I am the resurrection, and the life: he that believeth in me, though he were dead, yet shall he live: 26 And whosoever liveth and believeth in me shall never die. Believest thou this?

Over and over again in Scripture we learn that we can have eternal life through faith in the blood of Jesus Christ. By asking the question; *"why will ye die"* he was telling us there is no good reason to die because he has offered life through his Son, the Lord Jesus Christ.

Choose life today!

Question 2
Where Are You Spiritually?

Genesis 3:9 And the LORD God called unto Adam, and said unto him, Where art thou?

This question comes from an interaction between God and the first man; Adam. Adam's wife Eve is tempted by the Serpent (Satan) to disobey the word of God. Unfortunately, she takes the bait and sins. Adam, knowing what his wife has just done, does the same and sin enters into the world of mankind through Adam. This is the simple and true story of the source of mankind's problems today; sin.

When God first created Adam, he created him without sin. Adam lived in harmony with God, being alive both physically and spiritually. When Adam sinned, he died spiritually that day and eventually he would die a physical death also. When he sinned, his spirit was no longer aligned to God's Holy Spirit and fellowship between them was broken.

Sin had an immediate impact on Adam and his wife and their relationship with their Creator. We read the following from Scripture; *Genesis 3:7 And the eyes of them both were opened, and they knew that they were naked; and they sewed fig leaves together, and made themselves aprons. 8 And they heard the voice of the LORD God walking in the garden in the cool of the day: and Adam and his wife hid themselves from the presence of the LORD God amongst the trees of the garden.*

All of a sudden Adam and Eve knew they were naked and feared their Creator. God did not create them to fear him; their sin caused their fear that day.

It was at this very moment of confusion and fear in the lives of his Creation that God asked Adam; *"Where art thou"*? It's not that God didn't know where Adam was. It was Adam himself who did not yet fully understand where he was in his spiritual relation with God. You see, Adam was now dead in trespasses and sin. Nothing would ever be the same again. And yet, in that very question, we see the Creator's concern for his children. In fact, he would soon tell them of the consequences of their sin and the way back to him.

That same God and Creator has reached down from Heaven in human form 2,000 years ago and is still asking people the same question; *"Where art thou"*? So, I will ask you today to consider that question; how is your relationship with the one who created you? Do you know him in a personal way through the Scriptures, or simply know him by reputation only?

Question 3
What Seek Ye?

John 1:38 Then Jesus turned, and saw them following, and saith unto them, What seek ye?

One day as Jesus was walking along two disciples followed Jesus as he went. When Jesus became aware of them, he turned to them and said: *"What seek ye"*? Their reply was rather simple; saying, we want to know where you are living. But Jesus knew their hearts, as he knows yours today. He knew that deep down inside these two disciples was a desire to learn more about the man who was being called the Lamb of God. And so, Jesus invited them with the simple invitation; *"Come and see"*.

What a key question we have from Jesus for us to consider. In life people seek so many things, from the unnecessary to the necessary. Maybe you have been seeking things in your life and have found them; fame and fortune, as it were. But having found these things you still experience a stirring in your soul for something else, something more. What you have found so far in life has still left an emptiness or a shallowness inside you...and you wonder, is this all there is to life?

Jesus offers you so much more. As he invited the disciples that day to *"Come and see"*, he invites you also. Listen to his words in another invitation that he still holds out to people today.

> *Matthew 11:28 Come unto me, all ye that labour and are heavy laden, and I will give you rest. 29 Take my yoke upon you, and learn of me; for I am meek and lowly in heart: and ye shall find rest unto your souls. 30 For my yoke is easy, and my burden is light.*

Perhaps you feel burdened in your heart today; life in some way has grown difficult or disappointing, and you don't know where to turn. You are stuck in the same spot doing the same thing and you can't seem to get off the proverbial merry-go-round of life. If that's you today, Jesus offers to bring rest to your soul. He will bring this rest as you spend time in the word of God getting to know him in a deeper, more intimate way. This rest can only come when you *Come and see,* and consider that question that Jesus asked 2000 years ago; *What seek ye*?

Question 4
Whom say ye that I am?

Matthew 16:15 He saith unto them, But whom say ye that I am?

One day Jesus was walking through the coasts of Caesarea Philippi when he asked his disciples a question. He said; *"Whom do men say that I the Son of man am"*? As Jesus always was doing when he asked a question, he was going somewhere with his line of thought. The disciples answered him and said some people think you are one of the Prophets of old. This is where Jesus brought his seemingly "innocent" question into focus. His follow-up question was the question not quite as easily answered; *"But whom say ye that I am"*?

With this one simple question Jesus got to the heart of faith. Faith is receiving truth, even when we don't fully understand all its implications. Faith is receiving that truth, and most importantly, acting upon it. This is what Jesus was trying to drive home to his disciples. One of the disciples that day, Simon Peter, answered the Lord correctly; *"Thou art the Christ, the Son of the living God"*.

This answer of Peter's is the key that unlocks a person's eternal destiny. Jesus is indeed the Christ, which is, the Messiah. He was the one God the Father promised would come *(Genesis 3:15)*; the one who would save the world from the penalty of sin by his sacrificial death on the cross and subsequent resurrection from the dead.

Please consider carefully this question Jesus posed to his disciples and make sure you answer it for yourself. The call to salvation by faith goes out to everyone...but each one must answer that call by themselves.

Question 5
Where is your faith?

Luke 8:25 And he said unto them, Where is your faith? And they being afraid wondered, saying one to another, What manner of man is this! for he commandeth even the winds and water, and they obey him.

It matters what you believe and who you believe in. We all know this from the common experiences we face in our lives. But when it comes to spiritual matters and matters of the soul and eternal life, we somehow think it doesn't matter! Nothing could be further from the truth.

In Luke's gospel we read the words; *"Where is your faith"*? Jesus had just miraculously calmed the stormy sea that he and his disciples were sailing through. Jesus was saying to them in effect; don't you know as long as I am with you, you are safe. In his presence, no one ever dies, for he is life itself. The disciples learned a great lesson that day; trust Jesus, put your faith in Jesus.

When it comes to matters of eternal life for your soul, it matters where your faith is. What or who are you trusting to get you to Heaven, safe and sound, through the storms of life? People with little or no faith in their Creator are often fearful people because they know that they don't know Jesus in a personal way. Jesus once said; *"And he said unto them, Why are ye so fearful? how is it that ye have no faith"? (Mark 4:40)*

Faith and trust go hand in hand. You trust someone you have faith in and you have faith in someone you trust. The Lord Jesus Christ is worthy of your trust and faith because he is *"Faithful and True" (Revelation 19:11).* Having died for you, he has proved his love and deserves your trust.

Faith in the Son of God and in his Word pleases God. As a matter of fact, the bible says; *But without faith it is impossible to please him:*

for he that cometh to God must believe that he is, and that he is a rewarder of them that diligently seek him. (Hebrews 11:6).

The bible says that we are saved (eternally) by God's grace (favor) through the exercise of our faith (belief and trust) in him, not by any good deed we have done *(Ephesians 2:8-10)*.

The Lord expects his children of faith *(Galatians 3:26)* to live by faith and thus please him and demonstrate to others what true faith is all about.

> *Romans 1:17 For therein is the righteousness of God revealed from faith to faith: as it is written, The just shall live by faith.*

Question 6
Wilt Thou Be Made Whole?

John 5:6 When Jesus saw him lie, and knew that he had been now a long time in that case, he saith unto him, Wilt thou be made whole?

In Jerusalem one day Jesus came across a certain man which had an infirmity for 38 years! This infirmity apparently affected his ability to walk, and he longed to be healed. And thankfully, Jesus did heal him that day!

Most of us can understand at least a little of what he was going through. You probably know someone who has struggled with an infirmity of spirit or body...and they long to be made whole. Maybe that person is you. Perhaps you are the person who has suffered for years and long for someone to do what Jesus did that day in Jerusalem. Does the bible offer any hope in this regard? Let's take a look at it. The Prophet Isaiah was proclaiming the future death of Jesus on Calvary's cross when he spoke these words:

Isaiah 53:5 But he was wounded for our transgressions, he was bruised for our iniquities: the chastisement of our peace was upon him; and with his stripes we are healed.

The claim of this Prophet is that by the death of Jesus Christ people have been offered healing. Since a person is both spirit/soul and body, what does this verse mean...what should I expect? In order to best understand this verse from the Bible we need to look at both the here-and-now and the hereafter.

The here-and-now of life; Healing of the inner being (spirit/soul)

As to a person's inner being of soul and spirit, Jesus speaks healing through his Holy Bible. The words of the Bible are pure, holy, wise and truthful. Putting your absolute trust in the words of God can bring wholeness to the inner being in this lifetime. Jesus understands that we sometimes feel overwhelmed by life and the troubles that it can bring. He once said to some of his disciples; *And he said unto them, Why are ye troubled? and why do thoughts arise in your hearts? (Luke 24:38)*

There is no "magic" to this peace and wholeness that Jesus offers. There is no one set "formula" to achieve the inner peace that Jesus bought with the stripes of the Roman whip. Here is what the Bible does instruct believers to do:

> *Philippians 4:6 Be careful for nothing; but in every thing by prayer and supplication with thanksgiving let your requests be made known unto God. 7 And the peace of God, which passeth all understanding, shall keep your hearts and minds through Christ Jesus.*

The first encouragement here is to not let your imagination run wild in anxious (*"careful"* ...full of care) thoughts. But the scripture doesn't stop there, as it instructs us to pray. It is in prayer that we can tell our loving Saviour all about our struggles. He understands because when he was in human form, he suffered many of the same troubles we do today. The Bible says that he was a *"man of sorrows"* and *"acquainted with grief"*. Don't ever forget that; Jesus understands because he was here and saw all the trouble that sin had wrought on his creation.

The here-and-now of life; Healing of the outer being (body)

Often it is the physical healing we are after; the body is in some form of "dis-ease" and needs wholeness or healing. There have been many times when the Lord has answered the prayers of his children and brought physical healing, and we thank the Lord for that. Please don't confuse genuine healing brought by the prayers of the faithful with the phony so-called faith-healers that you hear about from time to time. There was a time in the early church (2,000 years ago) that God gave special healing powers to certain men that he called Apostles, but their ministry is long since over and has been replaced by Pastors and Evangelists in local churches. So, if you are sick or diseased in the body, call your Pastor or a fellow-believer and ask them to pray for you; who knows what the Lord may do (*2 Samuel 12:22*)!

The hereafter; Healing of both the inner and the outer being

The reality of this life is that it is full of trouble (*Job 5:7*) and the years are all too few; like a tale that is told (*Psalm 90:9*). Blink too long and your life is almost over. I don't say this to be pessimistic but rather to put this life in perspective when it comes to the (eternal) afterlife. Remember, life is short...eternity is long! So, I would like to examine eternal life with respect to the healing that Jesus offers.

Listen to the encouraging words that the Apostle Paul writes to the believers in a city known as Corinth:

> *2Corinthians 4:16 For which cause we faint not; but though our outward man perish, yet the inward man is renewed day by day. 17 For our light affliction, which is but for a moment, worketh for us a far more exceeding and eternal weight of*

glory; 18 While we look not at the things which are seen, but at the things which are not seen: for the things which are seen are temporal; but the things which are not seen are eternal.

Paul, in the verses above, acknowledges the brevity of life, and then quickly weighs the value of this life in the balance of eternity. He concludes that eternity is far more important than the 70 to 80 years of life we have here and now.

Now why would he do that? Because he knows something about the life to come for the believer who has trusted Jesus Christ as their Saviour. He wrote about it in another letter to the church at Corinth, called First Corinthians. In that letter the Apostle tells of a time in the future when Christ will return in the sky to call his (true) church of believers home to Heaven. This is often called the Rapture or the "Catching Away". When the Lord returns for this purpose, he is going to change our mortal corruptible bodies into immortal and incorruptible bodies. In these new bodies we receive our true healing in both the inner person and the outer person; in other words, our spirit and soul gets a brand-new heavenly body to live in forever! Listen to the words of the Apostle as he writes about this:

1Co 15:50 Now this I say, brethren, that flesh and blood cannot inherit the kingdom of God; neither doth corruption inherit incorruption. 51 Behold, I shew you a mystery; We shall not all sleep, but we shall all be changed, 52 In a moment, in the twinkling of an eye, at the last trump: for the trumpet shall sound, and the dead shall be raised incorruptible, and we shall be changed. 53 For this corruptible must put on incorruption, and this mortal must put on immortality. 54 So when this corruptible shall have put on incorruption, and this mortal shall have put on immortality, then shall be brought to pass the saying that is written, Death is swallowed up in victory. 55 O death, where is thy sting? O grave, where is thy victory? 56 The sting of death is sin; and the strength of sin is the law. 57 But thanks be to God, which giveth us the victory through our Lord Jesus Christ. 58

Therefore, my beloved brethren, be ye stedfast, unmoveable, always abounding in the work of the Lord, forasmuch as ye know that your labour is not in vain in the Lord.

If you want complete and everlasting healing put your trust in the gospel of Jesus Christ; the Good News that Jesus died, was buried and rose again the third day, according to the scriptures.

Question 7
Why Do Ye Not Believe Me?

John 8:45 And because I tell you the truth, ye believe me not.
46 Which of you convinceth me of sin? And if I say the truth, why do ye not believe me?

One of the many things that set Jesus apart from all others was his truthfulness. He once told his disciples; *"Nevertheless I tell you the truth"*. In another place in scripture, he said; *"I am the truth"*. All that Jesus ever did or said was rooted in truth. Truthfulness is the only way a fruitful relationship can be built, and without it, any relationship begins to crumble in mistrust. This is why truthfulness is so important, and this is why Jesus always told us the truth, whether painful or joyful.

Jesus spoke many words when he was here on earth and he left us many more words through his Holy Spirit, the true author of the Holy Bible. Jesus spoke of Heaven and Hell, his Father in Heaven, and the new Comforter (Holy Ghost) that he would send when he returned to Heaven. He also spoke of a time that would come upon all humankind in the future that would try their hearts like never before; calling this, the *great tribulation (Matthew 24)*.

Perhaps the greatest truth that Jesus spoke about was Heaven and Hell, for Heaven or Hell awaits every person who has ever lived. According to Jesus, there is a Hell to be avoided; a place of fire and torments (*Luke 16:23*). Jesus also declared that the pathway to Hell was wide and easy for people to find. To find the pathway to Hell all one needs to do is reject the Word of God and the gospel of Jesus Christ. But the good news is that all someone needs to do to find the pathway to Heaven is to believe the Word of God and the gospel of Jesus Christ...by faith. The Bible says that we are all children of God by faith in Jesus Christ (*Galatians 3:26*).

Jesus paid the price on Calvary's cross for the sin of the whole world and he offers each person the gift of eternal life. And Jesus said; *"Nevertheless I tell you the truth"*.

Question 8
Will Ye Also Go Away?

John 6:67 Then said Jesus unto the twelve, Will ye also go away?

Our Creator desires to have fellowship (friendship) with those he created. God created Adam in his own image and spoke with him prior to Adam sinning in the Garden of Eden. In *John 15:15* Jesus told his disciples that he considered them to be friends.

When we were young it was easy to believe in a Creator God. Adults we trusted told us so and everywhere we looked we could see evidence of his intelligent design in the world around us. Someone once said that a young person needs to be educated out of a belief in God, and that is certainly true for some people. As we get older it doesn't seem "enlightened" to believe the way we did when we were a child. We hear the lies of evolution and are afraid to stand our ground in the simple faith we once had. And so many of us have given up on God or faith and moved on to other things in life.

Jesus understood that the cares of this world and the deceitfulness of our riches *(Matthew 13:21-22)* could lead us in a direction away from him. But his heart's desire is to have a personal relationship with you now through his Holy Spirit and his Word. This is why he still calls out to people today; *Come unto me* he beckons in his word.

Maybe you have wandered far from the faith your once had in the Almighty God and his Son, Jesus Christ. It is not too late to find your way back to him. **Hebrews 10:22** says in part; *Let us draw near with a true heart in full assurance of faith.* If you reach out to God in true humble faith he will restore your faith and show great and wonderful things from his Holy Word.

Question 9
What is the value of your soul?

Jesus once asked the question; *For what shall it profit a man, if he shall gain the whole world, and lose his own soul? (Mark 8:36).* When Jesus spoke those words, he was trying to get his disciples and the people around him to consider the value of their soul, and to weigh in the balance, worldly pursuits and heavenly pursuits. Don't miss Heaven because you focused all your thoughts on the world.

There are many pursuits in life that occupy our time. Jesus was telling the people that some things are more important than others; they are not all equal. As a matter of fact, the most important pursuit is the care of your soul. Jesus believed the human soul was so valuable that he died to give it eternal life... Jesus died to offer you and I eternal life; this is how much Jesus valued your soul...valued, you!

Perhaps you have pursued something or someone in your life and you have been left feeling empty or even hopeless. Never forget the value Jesus placed on your soul when he willingly gave up his life to redeem it. You have value and worth in Christ. Jesus offers you another choice in life; seek him. Here is the full account of the events that day.

Mark 8:34 And when he had called the people unto him with his disciples also, he said unto them, Whosoever will come after me, let him deny himself, and take up his cross, and follow me. 35 For whosoever will save his life shall lose it; but whosoever shall lose his life for my sake and the gospel's, the same shall save it. 36 For what shall it profit a man, if he shall gain the whole world, and lose his own soul? 37 Or what shall a man give in exchange for his soul?

Jesus is looking for people everywhere to follow him and learn of him. His prophet Micah said; *He hath shewed thee, O man, what is good; and what doth the LORD require of thee, but to do justly, and to love mercy, and to walk humbly with thy God?* Be careful how you invest your life. Weigh out the value of your soul now before it's too late. Remember, the value of your soul is worth far more than any pursuit the world has to offer, no matter how good or noble it may seem. And by the way, if you invest your life in Christ, he will make your life more satisfying than anything this world has to offer.

Question 10
Does Thou Believe on the Son of God?

John 9:35 Jesus heard that they had cast him out; and when he had found him, he said unto him, Dost thou believe on the Son of God?

> *Amazing grace, How sweet the sound*
> *That saved a wretch like me.*
> *I once was lost, but now I am found,*
> *Was blind, but now I see.*
> *(Amazing Grace; John Newton, 1779)*

One day Jesus healed a man that was blind from his birth. As you might well imagine, the former blind man was ecstatic at being able to see for the first time in his life! This caused quite a stir among his neighbors who knew that he was blind all his life. The religious Jewish leaders did not believe that he had been blind, and that Jesus had healed him. As religious leaders often do when their corner on religious authority is threatened, the Pharisees tried to cause trouble for the young man and his family for having received the blessing of God without their input. When the Pharisees did not get the answer, they wanted from the young man or his family *"they cast him out"* from the Synagogue.

Here is where we pick up the story as Jesus finds the young man and asks him the all-important question about his faith.

John 9:35 Jesus heard that they had cast him out; and when he had found him, he said unto him, Dost thou believe on the Son of God?

Jesus knows the condition of this man and he knows what the Pharisees have just done to him as a result of his being healed by Jesus. Rather than dwell on the man's current predicament before the Pharisees, Jesus gets right to the important issue confronting this man; did he believe on the Son of God.

As the man was honest with Jesus in his reply, so too should we be. If there is something you don't understand about God, ask him. Here is the rest of the account that day.

John 9:36 He answered and said, Who is he, Lord, that I might believe on him? 37 And Jesus said unto him, Thou hast both seen him, and it is he that talketh with thee. 38 And he said, Lord, I believe. And he worshipped him.

Jesus plaining declared himself to be the very Son of God, and therefore equal with God. Of course, this is so because Jesus is God. The young man finds the only good response to the Lord's statement; faith and worship in the one true God.

Jesus is waiting today for more responses such as the young man's all those years ago. Jesus desires you to believe on him and to worship him as the only Saviour of the world. Don't delay, reach out to him by faith today and he will respond in a way only he can!

Appendix 1
What's Next For Humanity

As I stated in the introduction to this book, mankind is inquisitive, desiring to know. This desire was a gift from God but has unfortunately caused some to err in searching out answers to their questions in many destructive ways. I have tried to demonstrate in this book that the answers to life's most important questions are found in the Bible; written by God himself, the Creator of mankind.

I thought it important to give the reader a glimpse of what the future holds for mankind. Many people write about the future, many plan for the future and many more simply wonder about the future. And we wonder; will the human race ever learn to live at peace with each other? Will we ever solve the human suffering and death problem? What will the future be like? What will my future be like? The Bible addresses these issues directly and truthfully, without holding back the truth from those who would know what the future holds.

The Future of Humanity

The near-term future for humanity is not bright. There is a time coming to planet earth that will be a time of great judgment from God. Jesus talked about this future in the Gospel of Matthew (chapter 24) when his own disciples asked about the future, saying, *"what shall be the sign of thy coming, and of the end of the world"*. He explained to them the great turmoil which was to come. Here are a few of the things that Jesus said would be coming to the people of earth:

- Spiritual deception
- Continual wars and rumors of wars
- Nations rising up against other nations
- Famines
- Pestilences

- Earthquakes in many places

Unfortunately, Jesus said that these events would be just *"the beginning of sorrows"*. He then went on to explain that even greater judgment would be coming in a time he described as *"great tribulation, such as was not since the beginning of the world to this time, no nor ever shall be"*. This future period is detailed in the last book of the Bible called, The Revelation or as some call it, the Apocalypse.

Global Government

For years those of us who would talk about the future world government were laughed at or simply dismissed as conspiracy theorists. Today, many of those same people now see that the conspiracy to form a world government was absolutely true. It doesn't take much research before you uncover the global new world order. The institutions are all around today; here is just a partial list:

1. The United Nations and all their offshoots
2. The World Bank
3. The Bank for International Settlement
4. The Central Banks of the world (Federal Reserve)
5. The International Monetary Fund
6. The World Health Organization

The controllers of these institutions have formed various think tanks and organizations that control much of what we see going on in the world. Organizations that were once only whispered about or denied altogether, have suddenly come to the forefront as the "hope" of society. Again, here is a very small list of some of those organizations who have taken it upon themselves to be our "masters and overlords".

1. The Council on Foreign Relations
2. The Tri-lateral Commission
3. The Club of Rome

4. The World Economic Forum
5. The Bilderberg Group
6. And of course, our old standby, the United Nations

These world-wide organizations work in a form of governing known as Public-Private-Partnerships. In other words, the governments of the world work with the large trans-national corporations and the tens of thousands of NGOs (Non-Government Organizations) to implement the policies of the world leaders. A fairly recent example of this was when former president Trump issued his so-called Operation Warp-speed to rush to market with the experimental mRNA jab.

The impact of the global banks (Central Banks) of the world cannot be overestimated. The "printing" of new money without the corresponding increase in new goods and services is causing the inflation we are experiencing in 2022. Governments turn to the Central Banks when they have over spent (deficit spending).

The book of Revelation discusses the formation of a Global Government under the control of a man known as the Antichrist, a pawn of Satan himself. Along with a world-wide religious leader known as the False Prophet, they will seek to control the world and usher in a period of global worship of Satan.

The Dragon and the Beast

> *Rev 13:4 And they worshipped the dragon which gave power unto the beast: and they worshipped the beast, saying, Who is like unto the beast? who is able to make war with him? 5 And there was given unto him a mouth speaking great things and blasphemies; and power was given unto him to continue forty and two months. 6 And he opened his mouth in blasphemy against God, to blaspheme his name, and his tabernacle, and them that dwell in heaven. 7 And it was given unto him to make war with the saints, and to overcome them: and power was given him over all kindreds, and tongues, and*

nations. 8 And __all that dwell upon the earth shall worship__ __him__, whose names are not written in the book of life of the Lamb slain from the foundation of the world.

The Dragon is identified for us in other parts of the Bible as representing Satan, the Devil. The Beast is identified in other parts of the Bible as the man known as the Antichrist. Notice, the Dragon wants to be worshipped, and this in fact, will be the final form of religion before the Lord's return. The Antichrist is Satan's future leader of the New World Order (Global Government) and he will also be worshipped for his great prowess as a leader of Nations.

This future world leader will hate the God of the Bible and anyone who puts their faith in God. This Antichrist will be given world-wide control over the peoples of the world and all the world will worship this man as a god.

It is at this time that God will send 21 separate judgments upon earth, known as the Seal, Trumpet and Vial judgments of Revelation 6 through 18. It will be a severe time and many, many people will die. At the end of a seven-year period of judgment God will battle with Satan and his armies and put down their rebellion at a place known as Armageddon. The Lord will lock up Satan in the bottomless pit *(Revelation 20:1-3)* and the Antichrist and the False Prophet in the Lake of Fire.

> *Revelation 16:16 And he gathered them together into a place called in the Hebrew tongue Armageddon.*
>
> *Revelation 19:20 And the beast was taken, and with him the false prophet that wrought miracles before him, with which he deceived them that had received the mark of the beast, and them that worshipped his image. These both were cast alive into a lake of fire burning with brimstone.*

It is during this time that Jesus Christ will rule and reign for 1,000 years on earth in a time known as the Millennial (thousand) Reign of Christ. Jesus will sit as King of kings over the kingdoms of the world.

Revelation 19:16 And he hath on his vesture and on his thigh a name written, KING OF KINGS, AND LORD OF LORDS.

After the thousand years are over, Christ will release the Devil from the Lake of Fire for one more brief period of time. It is at this time that Satan gathers together another army in an attempt to overthrow the true King, Jesus Christ. The Lord will very quickly put down this final rebellion and throw Satan into the Lake of Fire where he will dwell for ever, without end.

Revelation 20:7 And when the thousand years are expired, Satan shall be loosed out of his prison,
Revelation 20:9 And they went up on the breadth of the earth, and compassed the camp of the saints about, and the beloved city: and fire came down from God out of heaven, and devoured them. 10 And the devil that deceived them was cast into the lake of fire and brimstone, where the beast and the false prophet are, and shall be tormented day and night for ever and ever.

Judgment Day Has Come

At this time Jesus will bring (lost) humanity before him in judgment at his Great White Throne. If you have received Jesus Christ as your Saviour by faith, you won't be at this Judgment. You have already made it to Heaven and your works were judged at the judgement seat of Christ *(Romans 14:10; 1 Corinthians 3:12-13; 2 Corinthians 5:10)*. Here is an important distinction; for born-again saved people your works are judged to determine how the Lord will reward you in Heaven, but your soul has already inherited the promised eternal life. If you have never received the Lord Jesus Christ as your Saviour you will end up at the Great White Throne judgment.

Revelation 20:11 And I saw a great white throne, and him that sat on it, from whose face the earth and the heaven fled away; and there was found no place for them. 12 And I saw the dead, small and great, stand before God; and the books were opened: and another book was opened, which is the book of life: and the dead were judged out of those things which were written in the books, according to their works. 13 And the sea gave up the dead which were in it; and death and hell delivered up the dead which were in them: and they were judged every man according to their works. 14 And death and hell were cast into the lake of fire. This is the second death. 15 And whosoever was not found written in the book of life was cast into the lake of fire.

Call upon the Lord Jesus Christ while there is still time. The Bible simply says; *Believe on the Lord Jesus Christ and thou shalt be saved, and thy house (Acts 16:31).*

Appendix 2
The Genesis 47 Prophecy

The Genesis 47 Prophecy

As I consider the condition of the world and the events going on in the USA in 2022, I see great turmoil. The Bible describes the world in which we live as *"this present evil world" (Galatians 1:4).* The Lord said *evil men and seducers shall wax worse and worse, deceiving, and being deceived (2 Timothy 3:13).* Truly, the days in which we live are just as the Bible said they would be; *This know also, that in the last days perilous times shall come (2 Timothy 3:1).* The Bible describes these days as days in which mankind would worship just about anything, rather than its Creator *(Romans 1:25)*. It describes a day in which there would be great confusion about sexuality **(Romans 1:26-27)** and a time of great violence, pride, lies and all sorts of wickedness *(Romans 1:29-32)*. And all of this should come as no surprise because we have turned our backs on the Creator and he has given people *over to a reprobate mind (Romans 1:28)*.

The events unfolding right now, and those that will come to maturity during the Seven-Year Tribulation on earth (see Appendix One), were laid out for us in the Bible some 3500 years ago in the book of Genesis. Let me describe for you this prophecy.

First, let's get our bearings about what was going on around B.C.1700 in the Middle East and surrounding lands:

- Jacob (also known as Israel) and his sons are living in the Promised Land of Canaan.
- Jacob's sons are angry with their brother Joseph and jealous of their father's special love for him.
- When an opportunity presents itself, they sell their brother Joseph into slavery in Egypt.

- After some time in Egypt, the Pharoah of Egypt has a dream which God gives the interpretation of, to Joseph.
- As a result of his interpretation, Joseph becomes an exalted leader in Egypt
- The dream is the prophecy of seven years of plenty in the land, followed by seven years of famine.
- All the land is in the midst of a seven-year famine. In type, this points to the seven-year tribulation which is soon to come upon earth, as we were warned about by Jesus in Matthew 24.
- When we pick up this account in Genesis 47 the seven years of plenty are past and they are in the midst of the seven years of famine.
- By examining the details of Genesis 47 we get a clear picture of the events that are happening in our world today, and that will fully unfold during the seven-year tribulation when God metes out 21 judgments upon earth.

The food fails (Genesis 47:13)

On the recent cover of the Economist Magazine, there is a picture of a bundle of wheat with little human skulls making up the flower of the wheat. The article on the inside is a discussion of world-wide food shortages and famines that have already begun, with more trouble on the way.

Genesis 47:13 And there was no bread...

In other words, there was a severe famine which had decimated the food supply in the land of Egypt and the surrounding lands. Famines are food shortages...often severe and for a long period of time. It makes for a desperate population. A famine can be caused by many factors; (1) severe weather like a drought (2) disease among crops or cattle (3) but it can also be purposeful...in order to overthrow an enemy in war where you starve your enemy out, or as a method to enslave or perhaps kill a population. But a famine can also be a judgment by God upon wickedness as we see during the seven-year Tribulation.

Henry Kissinger once said; *"Control the oil and you control nations; control the food and you the control people"*. The Biden administration announced recently in 2022 that it would expand a program that pays farmers to leave land fallow, part of a broader, government-wide effort to cut greenhouse gas emissions in half by 2030. The new initiative will incentivize farmers to take land out of production by raising rental rates and incentive payments. This will contribute to food shortages in the near future.

Farmland in this country is being purchased and placed in the hands of those who may not have the best interest of the population in mind. The largest private owner of farmland in the USA is Bill Gates with over 240 thousand acres of farmland. China has spent billions of dollars buying tens of thousands of acres of US farmland.

The Climate Change agenda of the globalist elites dictates the reduction of meat production because its (so-called) carbon footprint is too big. The recent bird flu scare caused the killing of millions of chickens. There have been well over a dozen disabling events at US food facilities, such as, fires and plane crashes, which will take food production capacity off line for some period of time; again, leading to future food shortages. Everyone has no doubt heard about the baby formula shortages of recent months and we all see shelves not as full as they used to be

As man does his best to ruin the food supply now, God will eventually send out the rider on the black horse in Revelation 6 to further destroy the food supply and usher in an even greater famine of judgment against the New World Order of Babylon.

> *Rev 18:8 Therefore shall her plagues come in one day, death, and mourning, <u>and famine</u>; and she shall be utterly burned with fire: for strong is the Lord God who judgeth her.*

The Money Fails

Genesis 47:15 And when the money failed...

Proverbs 22:7 The rich ruleth over the poor, and the borrower is servant to the lender.

The USA, and the world at large, are servants to the lender right now...the lender sometimes being foreign governments, but most often it is that creature we lovingly call the Federal Reserve Bank (a Central Bank). Money is the means by which people carry out transactions in a simple way, without the need of bartering for goods or services, as in years past. Governments, with the cooperation of the Central Banks, spend way more than then they have. The only way to make up the difference for this overspending is to tax its citizens more, or borrow it. It turns out that borrowing is easier for governments to do, so they borrow it, largely from the Central Bank (who created it out of nothing and lend it to us at an interest rate. I call this is a Luciferian Debt System which is enslaving the nations of the world).

Genesis 47:15 talks about the money failing. One way in which money fails is when the form of money we use loses its value. We see the currencies of today beginning to fail all around us. Money fails when people lose trust in its value. People lose trust in its value during periods of time we call Inflation. Remember, the cause of inflation today is simple; deficit spending by the government...that is, borrowing money from the Federal Reserve that we don't otherwise have. Let me make it clear as clear can be; inflation is caused by printing too much money! This creates an excess of money without the corresponding increase in goods or services, and people quickly begin to figure out the money isn't worth what it was. Here is a simple example of the effect of inflation; in 1822 a one-ounce gold coin was worth $19.39. With that you could go out and buy a nice tailor-made suit, a new pair of shoes and have enough money left over for a nice dinner. In 2022 you could take a one once gold coin (valued at about $1,900), go out and buy a nice tailor-made suit, a new pair of shoes and a nice dinner. You can't do that with $19.39...that's inflation.

Today the USA's national debt is about $30 trillion. Every year we, and other governments around the world, add to their national debt by spending more than they take in. This is what causes inflation. This is not sustainable and will require a new form of government-controlled currency in the future.

By the way, the Lord had a great plan to keep inflation in check. It was called the year of Jubilee. Every 50 years all debts would be cancelled and everything would be renegotiated. This allowed the money supply to contract which kept inflation from going crazy.

> *Lev_25:10 And ye shall hallow the fiftieth year, and proclaim liberty throughout all the land unto all the inhabitants thereof: it shall be a jubile unto you; and ye shall return every man unto his possession, and ye shall return every man unto his family.*

The US and other world economies used to use gold as a means of stopping the money supply from going inflationary, but today we have a Luciferian debt system called fiat currency (money created out of nothing and backed by nothing) and the future calls for more electronic currencies, block chain transactions and eventually, the mark of the beast *(Revelation 13:17-18)*.

The bottom line...the money will fail. And out rides the black horse rider of *Revelation 6:5-6; "A measure of wheat for a penny, and three measures of barley for a penny..."*. In the Bible, a penny was a day's wage! With inflation running rampant, and government-imposed price controls being discussed right now, you can see the set-up for what will take place in the near future; scarcity of food and high inflation for what is left.

Money never has been the answer to man's problems or happiness, and make no mistake, the money will fail. The rich rulers of this world will have their day in the court of Jesus one day. But in the meantime, God is going to destroy their gods of money and power in the very near future.

> *James 5:1 Go to now, ye rich men, weep and howl for your miseries that shall come upon you. 2 Your riches are corrupted, and your garments are motheaten. 3 Your gold and silver is cankered; and the rust of them shall be a witness against you, and shall eat your flesh as it were fire. Ye have heaped treasure together for the last days.*

> *Zephaniah 1:18 Neither their silver nor their gold shall be able to deliver them in the day of the LORD'S wrath; but the whole land shall be devoured by the fire of his jealousy: for he shall make even a speedy riddance of all them that dwell in the land.*

The Means of middle-class wealth creation is destroyed

Genesis 47:17 And they brought their cattle...

Cattle and land were the basic means of production in those days, as they created wealth for families, lifting them out of poverty and into the middle class of wealth. This would relate to the small businesses and the middle-class worker today. In this country, and around the world, the middle class is losing its ability to pay their bills and save money for the proverbial "rainy day". The means of production is being destroyed by the run-a-way costs and the restrictions on supply; from oil restrictions and the corresponding rise in gas prices, to other forms of energy costs. We truly see the poor getting poorer and rich getting richer. More and more average people are relying on the government to supply their needs for them as the means of production gets squeezed out by inflation and increasing regulations for things like Climate Change.

When the government takes out the means of production, it leads to more enslavement of the average citizen (look at Fascism,

Communism, Democratic Socialism and their utter failure to help working families of the past). When you destroy the middle class in a society, you get more poor and more rich people. The wise writer of the book of Proverbs said; *Remove far from me vanity and lies: give me neither poverty nor riches; feed me with food convenient for me: Lest I be full, and deny thee, and say, Who is the LORD? or lest I be poor, and steal, and take the name of my God in vain (Proverbs 30:8).*

Genesis 47:19 Slavery/Servitude

> *Wherefore shall we die before thine eyes, both we and our land? buy us and our land for bread, and we and our land will be servants unto Pharaoh: and give us seed, that we may live, and not die, that the land be not desolate.*

In the future Tribulation to come, when the food fails and the money fails and the means of production fails for the average middle-class person, people will be desperate and ready to receive the mark of the beast in order to eat and live *(Revelation 13:16-18).*

Genesis 47:20 The Government Owns the Farm

> *Genesis 47:20 And Joseph bought all the land of Egypt for Pharaoh; for the Egyptians sold every man his field, because the famine prevailed over them: so the land became Pharaoh's.*

In the future, the world government (a Socialistic, Public Private Partnership) will control the food, the means of production and the people themselves. This Babylon System of the New World Order will be involved in the production of so much of the world's merchandise:

> *Revelation 18:12 The merchandise of gold, and silver, and precious stones, and of pearls, and fine linen, and purple, and*

silk, and scarlet, and all thyine wood, and all manner vessels of ivory, and all manner vessels of most precious wood, and of brass, and iron, and marble, 13 And cinnamon, and odours, and ointments, and frankincense, and wine, and oil, and fine flour, and wheat, and beasts, and sheep, and horses, and chariots, <u>and slaves, and souls of men</u>.

Genesis 47:21 Off to the cities...

The final stage being set is for control over the people and their very lives; from the energy they consume to the health care they receive. The Technocrat leaders of today are working hard on the technology that will allow them to control the very goods and services you consume on a daily basis.

> *Genesis 47:21 And as for the people, he removed them to cities from one end of the borders of Egypt even to the other end thereof.*

> *Isaiah 5:8 Woe unto them that join house to house, that lay field to field, till there be no place, that they may be placed alone in the midst of the earth!*

Over the years there has been a mass migration into cities. Today over 4 billion people live in urban areas. The antichrist and his kings will love it to be so because it is easier to control the population and the supply of goods and services and energy. Just look what they have done in the large cities of the world as a result of what they have called the Global Pandemic. Look at Shanghai, where 24 million people have been forcibly locked down in their high-rise apartments for weeks on end...all in the name of medical health and avoiding another "pandemic".

Unfortunately, our government, along with the other major governments of the world, are attempting to usher in the UN World Health Organization as **"the"** governing body when we have another (so-called) pandemic. Don't kid yourself, they can come up with another pandemic anytime they wish… and if they do, you just might find that you may be locked up in some fashion too. Now some of you may think this conspiracy talk…and it is. But in the bible the word conspiracy is used of <u>true collusion</u> among individuals, not false.

Look, all these things are the plans of the New World Order and UN Agenda 2030, along with the Great Reset of the World Economic Forum which just met in June 2022 in Switzerland to plan our lives for us. Satan will use this structure to begin to put together his government with the antichrist at its head. But remember, as God brings judgment upon the earth in the future, he is in control. He can knock out the globalist's plans and devices anytime he wishes.

In the book of Job, we find a picture of the Great Tribulation. In it we read the following words; *Job 5:12 He disappointeth the devices of the crafty, so that their hands cannot perform their enterprise. 13 He taketh the wise in their own craftiness: and the counsel of the froward is carried headlong.*

More Taxation by the world's government

> *Genesis 47:23 Then Joseph said unto the people, Behold, I have bought you this day and your land for Pharaoh: lo, here is seed for you, and ye shall sow the land. 24 And it shall come to pass in the increase, that ye shall give the fifth part unto Pharaoh, and four parts shall be your own, for seed of the field, and for your food, and for them of your households, and for food for your little ones. 25 And they said, Thou hast saved our lives: let us find grace in the sight of my lord, and we will be Pharaoh's servants.*

The government's servants now pay another tax; this time a 20% (1/5th) tax of all the produce of crops. Today, and in the future, the Bible says that one who would be prone to increasing taxes on the world's middle-class population would enter the government of the

Antichrist (Babylon's New World Order). We read in the prophet Daniel these words; ***Then shall stand up in his estate a raiser of taxes in the glory of the kingdom: but within few days he shall be destroyed, neither in anger, nor in battle (Daniel 11:20)***. This will be a world-wide tax as we saw when Jesus came to earth the first time *(Luke 2:1)*. A prime candidate for a world-wide tax right now would be some form of carbon or energy tax.

We see this Genesis 47 prophecy unfolding all around us now. This tells me that the Lord's return is growing ever nearer. Are you ready to meet your God? Where is your faith today? What are you trusting in to see you into Eternity? Don't rely on good luck or good works. Don't chance your soul on your good reputation or church denomination. The only way to Heaven above remains the Lord Jesus Christ, who said; *I am the way, the truth, and the life: no man cometh unto the Father, but by me (John 14:6).*

Your Future

So many of us want to know what happens to me when I die. It is perhaps the most obvious and important question of them all. The answer from the Bible is...it depends. It depends on what you do today with the Gospel of Jesus Christ (the death, burial and resurrection of Jesus Christ) by faith.

> ***John 3:36 He that believeth on the Son hath everlasting life: and he that believeth not the Son shall not see life; but the wrath of God abideth on him.***

If you have never believed on the Son of God for everlasting life, the wrath of God abides on you. This will all come out on Judgment Day. The Bible clearly says; ***And as it is appointed unto men once to die, but after this the judgment: (Hebrews 9:27).***

Here is the true scene of Judgment Day...

> ***Rev 20:11 And I saw a great white throne, and him that sat on it, from whose face the earth and the heaven fled away; and there was found no place for them.***

Here is Jesus upon his throne in Heaven preparing to judge individuals...it is Judgment Day. There is no earth to support you now, only Jesus, as the earth and the (first) heaven have fled away before him.

12 And I saw the dead, small and great, stand before God; and the books were opened: and another book was opened, which is the book of life: and the dead were judged out of those things which were written in the books, according to their works.

Each person, small or great, must now give an account before the great Creator. There will be no exceptions now. Because these have rejected the Gospel of Jesus Christ in life, they now stand ready to be judged according to their works. But their eternal judgment was already determined by their rejection of the Son of God. All that is left is for God to make his righteous judgment as to the punishment for rejecting Christ and for whatever works you had done in your lifetime.

13 And the sea gave up the dead which were in it; and death and hell delivered up the dead which were in them: and they were judged every man according to their works.

There will be no place to hide in that day. There will be no place to escape God's judgment.

14 And death and hell were cast into the lake of fire. This is the second death.

The terror of the second death in the lake of fire has come. Even death and hell cannot shield you from this terrible day.

15 And whosoever was not found written in the book of life was cast into the lake of fire.

The only escape is to have your name written in the book of life. In this book are the names of all those who lived and trusted Jesus Christ as their Saviour and put their faith in his Gospel. In the end, this is all that will matter.

For a further discussion of how you too can have your name written in the book of life, please see the next and final appendix.

Appendix 3
What is biblical salvation?

I think it important to lay before you the biblical answer to the questions; "What is salvation, what am I being saved from and where is this salvation found"?

When Adam sinned in the Garden of Eden, he allowed that sin to enter this world. This sin brought with it corruption and ultimately death. While Adam allowed sin to enter, each one of us sins all on our own; there is not one exception to that, save the perfect sinless Saviour, Jesus Christ.

> *Romans 5:12 Wherefore, as by one man sin entered into the world, and death by sin; and so death passed upon all men, for that all have sinned:*

Our sin separates us from the Holy God in Heaven and he will not allow any sin to infect his glorious Home. God created Hell for the Devil and his angels. Unfortunately, Hell has enlarged itself and those rejecting the free gift of salvation through faith in Jesus Christ will find themselves in Hell, followed by the Lake of Fire. Not only does our sin separate us from God now but most importantly, it separates us in Eternity to come.

> *Revelation 20:14 And death and hell were cast into the lake of fire. This is the second death. 15 And whosoever was not found written in the book of life was cast into the lake of fire.*

This is the very reason Jesus died on the cross at Calvary; to save mankind from the penalty of sin and to offer eternal life through Jesus Christ our Lord. This is the Good News of Gospel of Jesus Christ from the Bible:

Grace can conquer sin:

> *Romans 5:21 That as sin hath reigned unto death, even so might grace reign through righteousness unto eternal life by Jesus Christ our Lord.*

Jesus died for sinners:

> *Romans 5:8 But God commendeth his love toward us, in that, while we were yet sinners, Christ died for us. 9 Much more then, being now justified by his blood, we shall be saved from wrath through him.*

God's desire is that all people receive this truth by faith and inherit eternal life. This gift of salvation is offered to all, no matter your skin color or ethnic background.

> *1Timothy 2:3 For this is good and acceptable in the sight of God our Saviour; 4 Who will have all men to be saved, and to come unto the knowledge of the truth.*

The Lord would have all to repent of their sin and turn toward him by faith.

> *Acts 20:21 Testifying both to the Jews, and also to the Greeks, <u>repentance toward God, and faith toward our Lord Jesus Christ</u>.*

We find a great summary of the doctrine (teaching) concerning salvation in the Book of Romans. Some have labeled this the **Romans Road to Salvation** because it lays out biblical salvation so clearly.

> *Romans 3:23 For all have sinned, and come short of the glory of God;*

> *Romans 5:8 But God commendeth his love toward us, in that, while we were yet sinners, Christ died for us.*

Romans 6:23 For the wages of sin is death; but the gift of God is eternal life through Jesus Christ our Lord.

Romans 10:9 That if thou shalt confess with thy mouth the Lord Jesus, and shalt believe in thine heart that God hath raised him from the dead, thou shalt be saved. 10 For with the heart man believeth unto righteousness; and with the mouth confession is made unto salvation. 11 For the scripture saith, Whosoever believeth on him shall not be ashamed. 12 For there is no difference between the Jew and the Greek: for the same Lord over all is rich unto all that call upon him. 13 For whosoever shall call upon the name of the Lord shall be saved.

The offer of salvation has been made by the sacrifice of Jesus Christ at the cross and his resurrection from the dead three days later. The choice is yours to make...no one will force you. But I can say from experience that if you *"Believe on the Lord Jesus Christ, and thou shalt be saved"* ...and you will never be sorry. Open the door of your heart to him...and he will come in.

Behold, I stand at the door, and knock: if any man hear my voice, and open the door, I will come in to him, and will sup with him, and he with me. (Revelation 3:20)